James P. Anglin

Pain, Normality, and the Struggle for Congruence: Reinterpreting Residential Care for Children and Youth

Pain, Normality, and the Struggle for Congruence: Reinterpreting Residential Care for Children and Youth has been co-published simultaneously as *Child & Youth Services*, Volume 24, Numbers 1/2 2002.

Pre-publication REVIEWS, COMMENTARIES, EVALUATIONS . . .

"Residential care practitioners, planners, and researchers will find much of value in this RICHLY DETAILED monograph. Dr. Anglin's work ADDS CONSIDERABLY TO OUR UNDERSTANDING OF THE RESIDENTIAL CARE MILIEU as a crucible for change, as well as a scaffolding of support that transects community, child and family."

James Whitaker, PhD
Professor of Social Work
The University of Washington, Seattle

The Haworth Press, Inc.

Pain, Normality, and the Struggle for Congruence: Reinterpreting Residential Care for Children and Youth

Pain, Normality, and the Struggle for Congruence: Reinterpreting Residential Care for Children and Youth has been co-published simultaneously as *Child & Youth Services*, Volume 24, Numbers 1/2 2002.

The Haworth Press, Inc.
New York • London • Oxford

The *Child & Youth Services*™ Monographic "Separates"

Below is a list of "separates," which in serials librarianship means a special issue simultaneously published as a special journal issue or double-issue *and* as a "separate" hardbound monograph. (This is a format which we also call a "DocuSerial.")

"Separates" are published because specialized libraries or professionals may wish to purchase a specific thematic issue by itself in a format which can be separately cataloged and shelved, as opposed to purchasing the journal on an on-going basis. Faculty members may also more easily consider a "separate" for classroom adoption.

"Separates" are carefully classified separately with the major book jobbers so that the journal tie-in can be noted on new book order slips to avoid duplicate purchasing.

You may wish to visit Haworth's website at . . .

http://www.HaworthPress.com

. . . to search our online catalog for complete tables of contents of these separates and related publications.

You may also call 1-800-HAWORTH (outside US/Canada: 607-722-5857), or Fax 1-800-895-0582 (outside US/Canada: 607-771-0012), or e-mail at:

docdelivery@haworthpress.com

Pain, Normality, and the Struggle for Congruence: Reinterpreting Residential Care for Children and Youth, James P. Anglin (Vol. 24, No. 1/2, 2002). *"Residential care practitioners, planners, and researchers will find much of value in this richly detailed monograph. Dr. Anglin's work adds considerably to our understanding of the residential care milieu as a crucible for change, as well as a scaffolding of support that transects community, child, and family." (James Whitaker, PhD, Professor of Social Work, The University of Washington, Seattle)*

Residential Child Care Staff Selection: Choose with Care, Meredith Kiraly (Vol. 23, No. 1/2, 2001). *"Meredith Kiraly is to be congratulated. . . . A lucid, readable book that presents the fruits of international experience and research relevant to the assessment and selection of child care workers, and which does so in a way that leads to practical strategies for achieving improvements in this important field. This book should be read by anyone responsible for selection into child care roles." (Clive Fletcher, PhD, FBPsS, Emeritus Professor of Occupational Psychology, Goldsmiths' College, University of London; Managing Director, Personnel Assessment Limited)*

Innovative Approaches in Working with Children and Youth: New Lessons from the Kibbutz, edited by Yuval Dror (Vol. 22, No. 1/2, 2001). *"Excellent. . . . Offers rich descriptions of Israel's varied and sustained efforts to use the educational and social life of the kibbutz to supply emotional and intellectual support for youngsters with a variety of special needs. An excellent supplement to any education course that explores approaches to serving disadvantaged children at risk of failing both academically and in terms of becoming contributing members of society." (Steve Jacobson, PhD, Professor, Department of Educational Leadership and Policy, University of Buffalo, New York)*

Working with Children on the Streets of Brazil: Politics and Practice, Walter de Oliveira, PhD (Vol. 21, No. 1/2, 2000). Working with Children on the Streets of Brazil *is both a scholarly work on the phenomenon of homeless children and a rousing call to action that will remind you of the reasons you chose to work in social services.*

Intergenerational Programs: Understanding What We Have Created, Valerie S. Kuehne, PhD (Vol. 20, No. 1/2, 1999).

Caring on the Streets: A Study of Detached Youthworkers, Jacquelyn Kay Thompson (Vol. 19, No. 2, 1999).

Boarding Schools at the Crossroads of Change: The Influence of Residential Education Institutions on National and Societal Development, Yitzhak Kashti (Vol. 19, No. 1, 1998). *"This book is an essential, applicable historical reference for those interested in positively molding the social future of the world's troubled youth." (Juvenile and Family Court Journal)*

The Occupational Experience of Residential Child and Youth Care Workers: Caring and Its Discontents, edited by Mordecai Arieli, PhD (Vol. 18, No. 2, 1997). *"Introduces the social reality of residential child and youth care as viewed by care workers, examining the problem of tension between workers and residents and how workers cope with stress." (Book News, Inc.)*

The Anthropology of Child and Youth Care Work, edited by Rivka A. Eisikovits, PhD (Vol. 18, No. 1, 1996). *"A fascinating combination of rich ethnographies from the occupational field of residential child and youth care and the challenging social paradigm of cultural perspective."* *(Mordecai Arieli, PhD, Senior Teacher, Educational Policy and Organization Department, Tel-Aviv University, Israel)*

Travels in the Trench Between Child Welfare Theory and Practice: A Case Study of Failed Promises and Prospects for Renewal, George Thomas, PhD, MSW (Vol. 17, No. 1/2, 1994). *"Thomas musters enough research and common sense to blow any proponent out of the water. . . . Here is a person of real integrity, speaking the sort of truth that makes self-serving administrators and governments quail."* *(Australian New Zealand Journal of Family Therapy)*

Negotiating Positive Identity in a Group Care Community: Reclaiming Uprooted Youth, Zvi Levy (Vol. 16, No. 2, 1993). *"This book will interest theoreticians, practitioners, and policymakers in child and youth care, teachers, and rehabilitation counselors. Recommended for academic and health science center library collections."* *(Academic Library Book Review)*

Information Systems in Child, Youth, and Family Agencies: Planning, Implementation, and Service Enhancement, edited by Anthony J. Grasso, DSW, and Irwin Epstein, PhD (Vol. 16, No. 1, 1993). *"Valuable to anyone interested in the design and the implementation of a Management Information System (MIS) in a social service agency. . ."* *(John G. Orme, PhD, Associate Professor, College of Social Work, University of Tennessee)*

Assessing Child Maltreatment Reports: The Problem of False Allegations, edited by Michael Robin, MPH, ACSW (Vol. 15, No. 2, 1991). *"A thoughtful contribution to the public debate about how to fix the beleaguered system . . . It should also be required reading in courses in child welfare."* *(Science Books & Films)*

People Care in Institutions: A Conceptual Schema and Its Application, edited by Yochanan Wozner, DSW (Vol. 14, No. 2, 1990). *"Provides ample information by which the effectiveness of internats and the life of staff and internees can be improved."* *(Residential Treatment for Children & Youth)*

Being in Child Care: A Journey Into Self, edited by Gerry Fewster, PhD (Vol. 14, No. 2, 1990). *"Evocative and provocative. Reading this absolutely compelling work provides a transformational experience in which one finds oneself alternately joyful, angry, puzzled, illuminated, warmed, chilled."* *(Karen VanderVen, PhD, Professor, Program in Child Development and Child Care, School of Social Work, University of Pittsburgh)*

Homeless Children: The Watchers and the Waiters, edited by Nancy Boxill, PhD (Vol. 14, No. 1, 1990). *"Fill[s] a gap in the popular and professional literature on homelessness. . . . Policymakers, program developers, and social welfare practitioners will find it particularly useful."* *(Science Books & Films)*

Perspectives in Professional Child and Youth Care, edited by James P. Anglin, MSW, Carey J. Denholm, PhD, Roy V. Ferguson, PhD, and Alan R. Pence, PhD (Vol. 13, No. 1/2, 1990). *"Reinforced by empirical research and clear conceptual thinking, as well as the recognition of the relevance of personal transformation in understanding quality care."* *(Virginia Child Protection Newsletter)*

Specialist Foster Family Care: A Normalizing Experience, edited by Burt Galaway, PhD, MS, and Joe Hudson, PhD, MSW (Vol. 12, No. 1/2, 1989). *"A useful and practical book for policymakers and professionals interested in learning about the benefits of treatment foster care."* *(Ira M. Schwartz, MSW, Professor and Director, Center for the Study of Youth Policy, The University of Michigan School of Social Work)*

Helping the Youthful Offender: Individual and Group Therapies That Work, edited by William B. Lewis, PhD (Vol. 11, No. 2, 1991). *"In a reader-friendly and often humorous style, Lewis explains the multilevel approach that he deems necessary for effective treatment of delinquents within an institutional context."* *(Criminal Justice Review)*

Family Perspectives in Child and Youth Services, edited by David H. Olson, PhD (Vol. 11, No. 1, 1989). *"An excellent diagnostic tool to use with families and an excellent training tool for our family therapy students. . . . It also offers an excellent model for parent training."* *(Peter Maynard, PhD, Department of Human Development, University of Rhode Island)*

Transitioning Exceptional Children and Youth into the Community: Research and Practice, edited by Ennio Cipani, PhD (Vol. 10, No. 2, 1989). *"Excellent set of chapters. A very fine contribution to the literature. Excellent text." (T. F. McLaughlin, PhD, Department of Special Education, Gonzaga University)*

Assaultive Youth: Responding to Physical Assaultiveness in Residential, Community, and Health Care Settings, edited by Joel Kupfersmid, PhD, and Roberta Monkman, PhD (Vol. 10, No. 1, 1988). *"At last here is a book written by professionals who do direct care with assaultive youth and can give practical advice." (Vicki L. Agee, PhD, Director of Correctional Services, New Life Youth Services, Lantana, Florida)*

Developmental Group Care of Children and Youth: Concepts and Practice, Henry W. Maier, PhD (Vol. 9, No. 2, 1988). *"An excellent guide for those who plan to devote their professional careers to the group care of children and adolescents." (Journal of Developmental and Behavioral Pediatrics)*

The Black Adolescent Parent, edited by Stanley F. Battle, PhD, MPH (Vol. 9, No. 1, 1987). *"A sound and insightful perspective on black adolescent sexuality and parenting." (Child Welfare)*

Qualitative Research and Evaluation in Group Care, edited by Rivka A. Eisikovits, PhD, and Yitzhak Kashti, PhD (Vol. 8, No. 3/4, 1987). *"Well worth reading. . . . should be read by any nurse involved in formally evaluating her care setting." (Nursing Times)*

Helping Delinquents Change: A Treatment Manual of Social Learning Approaches, Jerome S. Stumphauzer, PhD (Vol. 8, No. 1/2, 1986). *"The best I have seen in the juvenile and criminal justice field in the past 46 years. It is pragmatic and creative in its recommended treatment approaches, on target concerning the many aspects of juvenile handling that have failed, and quite honest in assessing and advocating which practices seem to be working reasonably well." (Corrections Today)*

Residential Group Care in Community Context: Insights from the Israeli Experience, edited by Zvi Eisikovits, PhD, and Jerome Beker, EdD (Vol. 7, No. 3/4, 1986). *A variety of highly effective group care settings in Israel are examined, with suggestions for improving care in the United States.*

Adolescents, Literature, and Work with Youth, edited by J. Pamela Weiner, MPH, and Ruth M. Stein, PhD (Vol. 7, No. 1/2, 1985). *"A variety of thought-provoking ways of looking at adolescent literature." (Harvard Educational Review)*

Young Girls: A Portrait of Adolescence Reprint Edition, Gisela Konopka, DSW (Vol. 6, No. 3/4, 1985). *"A sensitive affirmation of today's young women and a clear recognition of the complex adjustments they face in contemporary society." (School Counselor)*

Adolescent Substance Abuse: A Guide to Prevention and Treatment, edited by Richard E. Isralowitz and Mark Singer (Vol. 6, No. 1/2, 1983). *"A valuable tool for those working with adolescent substance misusers.'' (Journal of Studies on Alcohol)*

Social Skills Training for Children and Youth, edited by Craig LeCroy, MSW (Vol. 5, No. 3/4, 1983). *"Easy to read and pertinent to occupational therapists." (New Zealand Journal of Occupational Therapy)*

Legal Reforms Affecting Child and Youth Services, edited by Gary B. Melton, PhD (Vol. 5, No. 1/2, 1983). *"A consistently impressive book. The authors bring a wealth of empirical data and creative legal analyses to bear on one of the most important topics in psychology and law." (John Monahan, School of Law, University of Virginia)*

Youth Participation and Experiential Education, edited by Daniel Conrad and Diane Hedin (Vol. 4, No. 3/4, 1982). *A useful introduction and overview of the current and possible future impact of experiential education on adolescents.*

Institutional Abuse of Children and Youth, edited by Ranae Hanson (Vol. 4, No. 1/2, 1982). *"Well researched . . . should be required reading for every school administrator, school board member, teacher, and parent." (American Psychological Association Division 37 Newsletter)*

Pain, Normality, and the Struggle for Congruence: Reinterpreting Residential Care for Children and Youth

James P. Anglin

Pain, Normality, and the Struggle for Congruence: Reinterpreting Residential Care for Children and Youth has been co-published simultaneously as *Child & Youth Services*, Volume 24, Numbers 1/2 2002.

The Haworth Press, Inc.
New York • London • Oxford

Pain, Normality, and the Struggle for Congruence: Reinterpreting Residential Care for Children and Youth has been co-published simultaneously as *Child & Youth Services*™, Volume 24, Numbers 1/2 2002.

The development, preparation, and publication of this work has been undertaken with great care. However, the publisher, employees, editors, and agents of The Haworth Press and all imprints of The Haworth Press, Inc. including The Haworth Medical Press® and Pharmaceutical Products Press®, are not responsible for any errors contained herein or for consequences that may ensue from use of materials or information contained in this work. Opinions expressed by the author(s) are not necessarily those of The Haworth Press, Inc. With regard to case studies, identities and circumstances of individuals discussed herein have been changed to protect confidentiality. Any resemblance to actual persons, living or dead, is entirely coincidental.

The Haworth Press, Inc., 10 Alice Street, Binghamton, NY 13904-1580 USA

Cover design by Lora Wiggins

Library of Congress Cataloging-in-Publication Data

Anglin, James P.
    Pain, normality, and the struggle for congruence : reinterpreting residential care for children and youth / James P. Anglin.
        p. cm.
        "Co-published simultaneously as Child & Youth Services, Volume 24, Numbers 1/2, 2002."
        Includes bibliographical references and index.
    ISBN 0-7890-2140-4 (hard : alk. paper) – ISBN 0-7890-2141-2 (pbk. : alk. paper)
        1. Group homes for children–British Columbia. 2. Group homes for youth–British Columbia.
I. Title: Reinterpreting residential care for children and youth. II. Child & youth services. III. Title.
HV745.B7A54 2003
362.73'2' 09711–dc21   2003007562

Indexing, Abstracting & Website/Internet Coverage

This section provides you with a list of major indexing & abstracting services. That is to say, each service began covering this periodical during the year noted in the right column. Most Websites which are listed below have indicated that they will either post, disseminate, compile, archive, cite or alert their own Website users with research-based content from this work. (This list is as current as the copyright date of this publication.)

Abstracting, Website/Indexing Coverage . . . . Year When Coverage Began

- **Child Development Abstracts & Bibliography**
  (in print & online) <www.ukans.edu> **1982**

- **CINAHL (Cumulative Index to Nursing & Allied Health Literature)**
  in print, EBSCO, and SilverPlatter, Data-Star, and PaperChase.
  (Support materials include Subject Heading List, Database Search
  Guide, and instructional video) <www.cinahl.com> **1997**

- **CNPIEC Reference Guide: Chinese National Directory**
  of Foreign Periodicals **1997**

- **Criminal Justice Abstracts** **1982**

- **Educational Research Abstracts (ERA) (online database)**
  <www.tandf.co.uk/era> **2002**

- **e-psyche, LLC <www.e-psyche.net>** **2001**

- **ERIC Clearinghouse on Elementary & Early Childhood**
  Education **1982**

- **Exceptional Child Education Resources (ECER), (CD-ROM**
  from SilverPlatter and hard copy) **1982**

(continued)

(continued)

*Special Bibliographic Notes related to special journal issues
(separates) and indexing/abstracting:*

- indexing/abstracting services in this list will also cover material in any "separate" that is co-published simultaneously with Haworth's special thematic journal issue or DocuSerial. Indexing/abstracting usually covers material at the article/chapter level.
- monographic co-editions are intended for either non-subscribers or libraries which intend to purchase a second copy for their circulating collections.
- monographic co-editions are reported to all jobbers/wholesalers/approval plans. The source journal is listed as the "series" to assist the prevention of duplicate purchasing in the same manner utilized for books-in-series.
- to facilitate user/access services all indexing/abstracting services are encouraged to utilize the co-indexing entry note indicated at the bottom of the first page of each article/chapter/contribution.
- this is intended to assist a library user of any reference tool (whether print, electronic, online, or CD-ROM) to locate the monographic version if the library has purchased this version but not a subscription to the source journal.
- individual articles/chapters in any Haworth publication are also available through the Haworth Document Delivery Service (HDDS).

To Gillian, my wonderful wife of thirty years, who shares a commitment to the well-being of all children and youth.

To Howard, Tessa, and Rebecca, our cherished children, who grew from teenagers into adults over the course of this study.

ABOUT THE AUTHOR

James P. Anglin is Professor and Director of the School of Child and Youth Care, University of Victoria, British Columbia, where he has been on faculty since 1979. He began his career as a front-line residential child and youth care worker and over the next decade held several coordinating, policy, and management positions. He has consulted and provided training in South Africa on "the transformation of the child and youth care system" with the national government's Inter-Ministerial Committee on Young People at Risk and the National Association of Child Care Workers. He has served as a technical adviser to the Adolescent Health Unit at the World Health Organization, is on the board of Reclaiming Youth International, and has presented papers, keynote addresses, and workshops in over 20 countries. In 1986 he joined FICE-International as a representative of FICE-North America and now serves as a representative for Canada. He has published in North American journals and international forums on a variety of child and youth care subjects, is Senior Associate Editor for the *Child and Youth Care Forum,* and serves on the editorial boards of *Child and Youth Services,* the *Journal of Child and Youth Work,* and *Reclaiming Youth at Risk.* He was coordinating editor for the text *Perspectives in Professional Child and Youth Care* (Haworth, 1990).

Pain, Normality, and the Struggle for Congruence: Reinterpreting Residential Care for Children and Youth

CONTENTS

Foreword

I am honored and delighted to be asked by Jim Anglin to write the foreword to this grounded theory text: *Pain, Normality, and the Struggle for Congruence*. The purpose of this grounded theory is to construct a theoretical framework that would explain and account for well-functioning staffed group homes for young people, that in turn could serve as a basis for improved practice, policy development, education and training, research, and evaluation. This study, using grounded theory methodology, was undertaken with the spirit of discovery in pursuit of a contemporary, grounded theoretical understanding of group home life and work. Its goal was to generate a theory that fits, works and is relevant from the actual practices of "good enough" group home life and work, as opposed to applying extant theory "as if" it would work. The reader will see that Anglin has achieved his goal with admirable success.

I and, I trust, the reader, will join in with Anglin's thrill and diligence in discovering his core category: "struggling for congruence in service of the children's best interests." It integrated the other categories of the theory in accounting for how a well-functioning group home is developed at all levels of home structure and for all levels of participants. Anglin shows, as in many other studies I have been involved in, that grounded theory discovers the relevant main concern of participants and how it is continually resolved, as opposed to imposing on the study before research a professional problem that often is not relevant for participants and for practice. Thus his theory, grounded in actual practice, will usefully and easily be applicable to improving practice and policy in other group homes, specifically with regard to establishing extrafamilial living, responding to pain-based behavior, and developing a sense of normality.

Although Anglin does not allow the extant literature to force itself on his theory beforehand, once the theory is formulated, he shows how the literature can be woven into his theory. Thus his theory is seen to both complement and extend other research. His grounded theory truly makes a scholarly contribution to the literature. Further, he shows how his theory has profound implica-

[Haworth co-indexing entry note]: "Foreword." Glaser, Barney G. Co-published simultaneously in *Child & Youth Services* (The Haworth Press, Inc.) Vol. 24, No. 1/2, 2002, pp. xv-xvi; and: *Pain, Normality, and the Struggle for Congruence: Reinterpreting Residential Care for Children and Youth* (James P. Anglin) The Haworth Press, Inc., 2002, pp. xv-xvi. Single or multiple copies of this article are available for a fee from The Haworth Document Delivery Service [1-800-HAWORTH, 9:00 a.m. - 5:00 p.m. (EST). E-mail address: docdelivery@haworthpress.com].

tions for child and youth care policy, education and practice–particularly interactional dynamics that work–and future research in these areas. Its conceptualizations are fully generalizable.

In sum, Anglin achieves and shows the power of a good grounded theory.

Barney G. Glaser, PhD, HonPhD
Mill Valley, California

Preface

DISCOVERING THE HEART OF DARKNESS

> When you have to attend to things of that sort, to the mere incidents of the surface, the reality–the reality, I tell you–fades. The inner truth is hidden. . . . But I felt it all the same. . . .
>
> –Marlow, in *Heart of Darkness* by Joseph Conrad (1990, p. 30)

This study of group homes for children and youth has been a voyage of discovery, one that included a vivid and startling dream that helped me to penetrate "mere incidents of the surface" and uncover a disturbing but largely hidden truth.

> I am walking across a snowy and frozen landscape. I am admiring the beauty of the snow-laden evergreen trees and the light patterns on the curves of the snow mounds between the trees. I am traversing a wide and flat expanse of snow, surveying the scene with an inner sense of curiosity and tranquility. Suddenly, I find myself falling downward, and I realise that I have broken through some thin ice. I had been walking across a frozen body of water without realizing it. My entire body is plunged into the frigid water, and air bubbles are streaming from my mouth as I gasp at being submerged and unable to breathe. Then I wake up, still feeling the after-effects of a shock-like reaction in my body. (Field note; November 13, 1999)

During the days immediately before this dream experience, I had been making intensive visits to three homes. Between visits, I had interviewed a number of residential workers and supervisors. On several occasions, I woke up very early in the morning with vague, visceral sensations of discomfort in reaction to what I had been experiencing. But this disturbing dream was the most profound "wake up call" that I had yet experienced. It seems that what had finally dawned on me at a somatic level was an experience of "embodied knowledge" (Benner & Wrubel, 1989, p. 42) in which I had grasped the meaning of the situation directly (but not abstractly) as a result of being personally engaged.

It did not take long to link this dream experience to my recent visits to several group residences and, in particular, my conversations with one staff mem-

[Haworth co-indexing entry note]: "Preface." Anglin, James P. Co-published simultaneously in *Child & Youth Services* (The Haworth Press, Inc.) Vol. 24, No. 1/2, 2002, pp. xvii-xviii; and: *Pain, Normality, and the Struggle for Congruence: Reinterpreting Residential Care for Children and Youth* (James P. Anglin) The Haworth Press, Inc., 2002, pp. xvii-xviii. Single or multiple copies of this article are available for a fee from The Haworth Document Delivery Service [1-800-HAWORTH, 9:00 a.m. - 5:00 p.m. (EST). E-mail address: docdelivery@haworthpress.com].

xvii

ber. It was immediately clear to me that the cold water in the dream represented pain and that the frozen landscape represented the busyness of daily routines that covered over the pain underneath the surface of group home life and work. And while this "inner truth" of pain had remained largely hidden from my conscious understanding for many months, I realized, like Marlow in Conrad's *Heart of Darkness* (1990), that I had "felt it all the same" (p. 30).

Analyzing the dream reminded me of a book of articles that I had read several years before entitled *Rivers of Pain, Bridges of Hope* (Davis, 1987). When I returned home from the week of site visits to the Valley Agency group homes, I pulled the book from my shelf and looked through it again. One of the first themes woven into Davis' discussion of residential group care was Victor Hugo's story of *Les Misérables*, and there were several references made to "darkness of the heart" (Davis, 1987, pp. 6-8). Davis says toward the end of his discussion, "At the micro-level, residential establishments often, and rightly so, go through their own revolutions when the "darkness" becomes intolerable for both clients and staff " (1987, p. 8).

Apropos to the reference to "revolutions," the day before the shocking dream I had heard from a relief staff member that a "riot" had occurred at one of the group homes several weeks before my arrival. Residents locked staff in the office, broke windows, and "trashed" the kitchen and other parts of the house. The police had to be summoned to restore order.

The words and images shared by this worker along with my direct participation in the homes had made a deep impression on me and awakened some insights that burst forth in the powerful dream experience. To this day, several years later, the dream images and the memories of the rapid process of interpretation that took place in the minutes after waking up early on that November 13th morning are readily accessible to me. Further, the phrase "heart of darkness" from Davis' writing echoed the title of Joseph Conrad's famous novel that I had not previously read. I did read it soon after this incident, and thus this haunting notion has since that time all-too-aptly captured for me the deep and pervasive pain lying at the heart of the residential care experience for both residents and staff members.

As the framework that emerged from this research study will reveal, responding to pain and pain-based behavior is the major challenge for carework staff in the group care settings studied. As residential child and youth practitioners, we would do well not to allow ourselves to become distracted by "the mere incidents of the surface" but to seek to discern the inner truth of the pain hidden within the daily reality of group home life and work and to find ways to guide the young residents and ourselves out of the heart of darkness and into a collective sense of normality. To do so requires nothing less than a ceaseless striving for appropriate consistency, reciprocity, and coherence throughout our child and youth care practice. It is this struggle for congruence in service of the children's best interests that provides the unifying theme for the creation of a nurturing and healing extrafamilial environment–a true "home for the heart" (Bettleheim, 1974).

Acknowledgments

For a multi-year research project, there are a great many people to thank. Above all, I want to begin by acknowledging the young residents and former residents of the group care programs involved in this study. You were the touchstones for this framework; yours is the pain at the heart of group home life and work, and you have inspired me to continue to advocate for better residential group care. May you experience unimaginable joy and success in the years ahead.

Of course, the young people in this study would not have experienced a growing sense of self-worth, normality, and hope without the child and youth care practitioners (careworkers, supervisors, and managers) who were prepared to live and work with them. For reasons of confidentiality, I am not able to mention each by name. You know who you are, and I thank each of you most sincerely for your trust and openness without which this study could not have been done.

My colleagues at the School of Child and Youth Care at the University of Victoria accepted my absences from the hallways of our building when I was engaged in field visits and drafting the manuscript. I cannot imagine a more supportive workplace or a better team of staff, faculty, and students with whom to work. Susan Larke, a doctoral candidate in the Faculty of Human and Social Development, suggested the term "pain-based behavior," and I am grateful to her for offering that particular wording. Diana Nicholson diligently proofread the entire manuscript, and Caroline Green created the marvelous graphic for the Framework Matrix. Thank you for your important contributions.

I want to give special acknowledgement to Dr. Sam Scully, a former Vice-President Academic at the University of Victoria; Dr. Jim McDavid, the former Dean of Human and Social Development; Dr. Anita Molzahn, current Dean of Human and Social Development; and Dr. Sibylle Artz, former Director of the School of Child and Youth Care, for their active support and encouragement over the course of this research process. Special mention needs to be made of Dr. Artz who made the completion of this book a goal for her term of Directorship. With her unflagging support, I made it under the wire.

Also, I wish to acknowledge a number of government officials who, all too often, work quietly and diligently behind the scenes, sharing a commitment to the well-being of children, youth, and their families, but whose important contributions frequently go unheralded. Over the course of this project, Ross

Dawson, Bernd Walter, Dr. Gregory Muirhead, Wayne Matheson, Jeremy Berland, Gerry Merner, Vaughan Dowie and Judy Hayes of the (now) Ministry of Children and Family Development gave the advice, approvals, and support essential for the success of significant portions of this research project. I gratefully acknowledge the financial assistance provided by the Ministry of Children and Family Development under contract #219800041.

I am most grateful to my editor at The Haworth Press, Dr. Doug Magnuson, who has been a strong supporter of this book since its early conception and whose patience, careful editing, insightful suggestions, and challenging comments have significantly strengthened the presentation of this text. Any remaining limitations or errors, however, are my sole responsibility.

Finally, I want to thank my mentor, guide, and patient supporter, my academic supervisor Dr. Harriet Ward, now of Loughborough University, who oversaw much of the research process associated with this publication. Long-distance academic supervision is a uniquely challenging endeavor, and I am convinced that no one could do it with more grace and diligence than Dr. Ward.

I can only hope that those who contributed to this study will consider the final product to be worthy of the time and effort they so generously invested in its creation.

J. P. A.
Victoria, BC

Introduction

A full and rigorous examination of the theoretical and empirical under-pinnings of residential group care with respect to their implications for current service policy, practice, and future research is long overdue and ought to receive the highest priority on the new century's emergent agenda.

–Jim Whittaker (2000, p. 60)

This inquiry sought to understand staffed group home life and work with children and youth in order to construct a framework for practice. In North America, the term "group home" is used to refer to extrafamilial care for young people in specially created residential settings that generally have between 4 and 8 residents. In the United Kingdom, such residences are commonly referred to as "children's homes" (Berridge & Brodie, 1998). It needs to be clarified at the outset that, while this study was pursued under the auspices of the School of Social Work at the University of Leicester, all of the residential settings involved in the research were located in British Columbia, Canada, where the author resides. However, relevant research and practice literature from both the United Kingdom and North America were reviewed in the preparation of the initial research proposal and will be referred to in a selective fashion at the end of this document when considering the significance and contribution of the resulting framework.

Several key terms deserve introduction here due to different usages and connotations on the two sides of the Atlantic. First, "children and youth" is the common phrase in North America for the full range of young people under the age of majority. There is not a negative connotation to the word "youth," and 14- to 24-year-olds are generally comfortable being referred to as "youth." In fact, the national organization of young people in the child welfare system in Canada is called the Federation of National Youth in Care Networks and "looked

[Haworth co-indexing entry note]: "Introduction." Anglin, James P. Co-published simultaneously in *Child & Youth Services* (The Haworth Press, Inc.) Vol. 24, No. 1/2, 2002, pp. 1-3; and: *Pain, Normality, and the Struggle for Congruence: Reinterpreting Residential Care for Children and Youth* (James P. Anglin) The Haworth Press, Inc., 2002, pp. 1-3. Single or multiple copies of this article are available for a fee from The Haworth Document Delivery Service [1-800-HAWORTH, 9:00 a.m. - 5:00 p.m. (EST). E-mail address: docdelivery@haworthpress.com].

http://www.haworthpress.com/store/product.asp?sku=J024
10.1300/J024v24n01_01

after" young people are commonly referred to and refer to themselves as "youth in care."

Another term utilized in North America that is not as prevalent in the United Kingdom is "program." As noted by Ainsworth and Fulcher (1981, p. 71), "there seems to be no generally accepted term in the context of British social care services which could be said to clearly parallel the North American meaning of programme." In the North American context, the term "program" is used to refer to the set of activities characteristic of a setting or service, thus it is frequently used as a synonym for the setting. For example, one frequently hears references to "the program" when a group home (or other type of social welfare service) is being referred to. Other such terms that may be subject to misunderstanding will be defined when they first occur in the text.

However, despite the differences in terminology, group homes and children's homes are situated similarly on the "residential care continuum." On the less formal or less professional side of group home care lies traditional foster care in which a single person or a couple take children or youth into their own homes and provide a surrogate family setting. On the more formal and professional side of the continuum are the institutional forms of care, including such residential programs or settings as mental health treatment centers, correctional detention units, and hospital wards.

The data for this study were collected over a 14-month period between October 1998 and December 1999, a time of heightened sensitivity to the rights of children, growing emphasis on accountability and outcome measurement in public and private services, and continuing fiscal pressures within governments in general.

In the first chapter, a brief overview of the history of residential care for young people and a number of the major contextual factors influencing contemporary group homes will be examined as a prelude to the presentation in Chapter 2 of the design and implementation of this study. Chapter 3 will introduce in "broad brush" or skeletal fashion the major elements of the theoretical framework that resulted from detailed comparative analysis of the extensive data gathered in this study. The main theme or core variable discovered to be most central and pervasive in group home life and work will be presented in Chapter 4, followed by a chapter on each of the three related major psychosocial processes or sub-themes also found to play key roles. The last two chapters will review selected literature through the lens of this framework with implications for residential child and youth care policy, education, practice and research.

Even a cursory review of the history of residential care for children and youth over the past thirty-five years reveals the impressive resilience of this form of service. Despite many rather scathing critiques on both sides of the Atlantic (e.g., Rae-Grant, 1971; Rubin, 1972; Steinhauer, 1991; Vail, 1966), revelations of institutional abuse (Bloom, 1992; Collins & Colorado, 1988; Levy & Kahan, 1991), and attempts to eliminate residential programs altogether (Cliffe & Berridge, 1992; Coates, Miller & Ohlin, 1978), residential care continues to play a significant role in virtually all child and family service systems. Further, while the absolute and per capita number of children in residential programs has decreased significantly on both sides of the Atlantic since the 1970s (Berridge & Brodie, 1998, p. 12; Anglin, 1994, p. 25), it appears that even most of the critics of residential care have accepted the inevitability of preserving at least some residential settings for the foreseeable future (e.g., Steinhauer, 1991). It would seem that, in relation to the child welfare service system as a whole, residential care is something like the tip of the iceberg that protrudes out of the water; if one tries to remove the tip, the iceberg moves upward to maintain its overall balance.

Over the past several decades, a number of major political and ideological movements and forces have placed considerable pressure on residential care programs. These have included deinstitutionalization, downsizing of government, a demand for accountability and quality assurance, mandating permanency planning, and a renewed emphasis on family support services.

Currently, there is a strong movement in favour of "homebuilder" and "family preservation" programs in North America (Brown & Hill, 1996). These programs seek to provide "short, sharp" interventions into the lives of client families in order to defuse a problem, often a crisis, without having to remove children from their own homes. Traditional residential care has come to be seen internationally, at least in the minds of many, as passé, misguided, overly intrusive, and exorbitantly expensive (Gottesman, 1994, pp. 2-9). Such current challenges and shifts in societal expectations and values have created a need to take a careful, in-depth look at the nature of residential care as a modality of child and youth care work, to provide some current information on how it operates, and to contribute knowledge and theoretical understanding grounded in current practice to the ongoing debate.

The quotation by Jim Whittaker (2000) prefacing this introduction urges that a "full and rigorous examination of the theoretical and empirical underpinnings of residential group care" be accorded "the highest priority on the new century's emergent agenda" (p. 60). It was in a spirit of appreciation of the vital importance of exploring the nature of residential life and work that this study was undertaken. It is hoped that what follows will make a modest but useful contribution to such an examination.

Chapter 1

Historical and Contemporary Issues in Residential Care for Children and Youth

No informed conclusion about the future of residential care can be reached without paying careful attention to the kinds of external changes that are likely to determine its scale and character. That, in turn, cannot be done satisfactorily without some understanding and appreciation of those forces that have shaped its history.

–Roy Parker (1988, p. 3)

The term "residential care" encompasses a wide and imprecise range of services. In some definitions it encompasses foster care, as young people are "in residence" in the foster homes for periods ranging from days to years. Other definitions use the term "residential" in direct opposition to "foster care." In this volume, the term will be used to cover the spectrum of "24-hour care" resources, from staffed homes for small groups of children to large congregate institutions such as residential schools and orphanages, but excluding foster care provided in families' own homes. Thus, in addition to group homes, the continuum of "residentiality" includes such services as detention facilities, mental health treatment centers, psychiatric wards, and boarding school residences.

This study was initiated to address the generally acknowledged need for a more in-depth understanding of residential life and residential work in children's residences (see Bullock, Little & Millham, 1993; Whittaker, 2000). This chapter will consider some of the larger historical and contemporary issues pertaining to the domain of residential care in general in order to set the group home study in context.

It is important to clarify at this point that the following selective review was undertaken in order to determine if the current study was warranted and to situate this research within the historical evolution of the residential care research

[Haworth co-indexing entry note]: "Historical and Contemporary Issues in Residential Care for Children and Youth." Anglin, James P. Co-published simultaneously in *Child & Youth Services* (The Haworth Press, Inc.) Vol. 24, No. 1/2, 2002, pp. 5-21; and: *Pain, Normality, and the Struggle for Congruence: Reinterpreting Residential Care for Children and Youth* (James P. Anglin) The Haworth Press, Inc., 2002, pp. 5-21. Single or multiple copies of this article are available for a fee from The Haworth Document Delivery Service [1-800-HAWORTH, 9:00 a.m. - 5:00 p.m. (EST). E-mail address: docdelivery@haworthpress.com].

http://www.haworthpress.com/store/product.asp?sku=J024
10.1300/J024v24n01_02

literature. Grounded theory, the method selected for this study, is primarily an inductive approach, and unlike more deductive approaches, one does not undertake a comprehensive review of the literature before initiating the study (Glaser, 1978, p. 31). At the same time, the researcher had an extensive work career in the field of child and youth care and was reasonably familiar with the residential care literatures in the United Kingdom and North America overall. It is important that the framework being sought in the grounded theory research process emerge from the actual research data to the greatest degree possible and not from prior formulations. As a result, after the study findings and emerging framework are explored, a more traditional review of selected relevant literature will be presented in relation to the emergent framework (see Chapter 8).

This chapter is organized around a number of the major themes found in the initial overview of relevant residential care literature from the United Kingdom and North America. One of the most fundamental questions raised pertains to whether the state should be involved in removing children from their homes at all and, if so, under what circumstances.

THE ROLE OF THE "STATE" IN RESIDENTIAL CARE

Social welfare policy and practice characteristic of the late 19th and first half of the 20th centuries has been under serious attack on both sides of the Atlantic during the latter part of the 20th century. This critique, sometimes referred to as "neo-conservative," combined with serious efforts to reduce government deficit spending, has brought about a profound rethinking of the role of the state. At the beginning of the 21st century, this questioning now appears to transcend political parties and is characteristic of the trend toward globalization and transnational corporate thinking. Even the provision of residential care for young people is necessarily subject to and greatly influenced by the various ideological forces that compete for ascendancy in societies over time (Gottesman, 1994, pp. 2-9).

In the field of child and youth care, Fox Harding (1991) suggests that we have entered into "a situation where there can be no certainty as to what the state should do, when it should do it, or how" (p. 3). In a useful overview of the major competing perspectives in child and youth care policy, Fox Harding identifies four major value orientations that characterize ways of thinking about the role of the state in parenting and the provision of child and youth care services–both residential and non-residential–namely, laissez-faire, protectionist, supportive, and radical.

Laissez-Faire

In the laissez-faire approach, parents are considered to be the best carers for children except in extreme cases of abuse and neglect. The biological bonds between natural parents and their children are considered to be vitally important to the proper attachment and socialization of children, and the recent historical efforts at "child saving" are considered to have been overzealous and likely to have caused more harm to children than they have prevented. According to this perspective, as Fox Harding points out, the central right of children is to have care and nurture provided by their natural parents. In brief, this perspective views the state as a poor parent, and maintains that substitute services should be kept to a minimum. This approach, characteristic of many conservative thinkers, also has the benefit of keeping state costs for child welfare services relatively low.

Protectionist

The protectionist stance is somewhat less parent-focused and is rather more concerned with the need to protect the child from the inadequacies of parents. The state is seen as being able to act in the role of a good parent due to its ability to be unbiased and to provide professionally competent services. The psychoemotional bonds with significant carers are understood to be more significant for a child than the biological relationship with parents. Children have the right to care and nurture, and the best care may be provided by a parent substitute. Services need to be quite extensive, requiring a relatively high investment of state funding.

Supportive

The supportive approach shares the laissez-faire perspective's emphasis on the importance of the biological bonds between the parent and child. However, more emphasis is placed upon the need for the provision of support services for the family. Social inequality is perceived as a major source of family problems, thus the need for some state support to families in order to care adequately for their children is recognized. The focus of service provision differs from the protectionist approach, with a much stronger emphasis on the need for family support services rather than substitute care arrangements. As with the laissez-faire approach, the basic right of the child is to live in the biological family. At the same time, whereas the laissez-faire orientation is minimalist in terms of cost, services, and intervention, the supportive approach has moderate to high expectations for expenditure and programs.

Radical

The fourth major perspective has a more radical view of the rights of the child and sees parents as being overly dominant in the lives of children generally. The state has an important role to play in ensuring sufficient autonomy for children and the focus is on their right to make choices. The autonomy and self-determination of children is more important than residing with biological or substitute parents, and independent living for youth is a favored option. The cost implications are low to moderate, as the focus is on the need for parent education services and independent living for young people unable to live at home.

THE SITUATION IN BRITISH COLUMBIA

In the early to mid-1990s in British Columbia, just prior to the inception of this study, the virtues of the laissez-faire, protectionist, and supportive orientations were actively debated, with the more right-wing political proponents championing the first (Magnusson, 1984), an independent judicial inquiry promoting the second (Gove, 1995a, 1995b, 1995c), and the Ministry of Social Services revising legislation and seeking to reorient the child welfare system more along the lines of the third (Ministry of Social Services, 1994). When the field research was undertaken for this study in late 1998 and throughout 1999, the protectionist philosophy was firmly in place as a result of the tabling of the report of the Commission of Enquiry into the Death of Mathew Vaudreuil (Gove, 1995a, 1995b, 1995c) and the strong groundswell of media, political, and professional support for its 118 recommendations. The general thrust of this major report was that no child should ever again die due to the abuse or neglect of a parent and that it was the responsibility of the state child welfare services to err on the side of protection rather than family support. For example, one recommendation stated:

> A social worker who considers that a child is in need of protection should apprehend and remove the child from an abusive or neglectful environment, and should not try to "second guess" what a judge will do once the case comes to court. (Recommendation 22, Gove, 1995b, p. 88)

This orientation, emphasizing the primacy of judicial assessment and intervention over the direct use of child welfare expertise, and articulated in the context of a highly visible public inquiry process, likely contributed directly to an approximately sixty percent increase in the number of children taken into care over the subsequent five-year period (Anglin, 2000).

While most ideological positions will accept that, under some circumstances at least, the state must intervene to remove and protect children for whom in-home protection is not possible, the evolution of residential care has witnessed a wide range of actual and potential purposes and functions for its use in addition to physical protection.

THE PURPOSES AND FUNCTIONS OF RESIDENTIAL CARE

There are always multiple purposes and functions for residential care. Over the last two centuries, it would appear that the emphases placed on the way residential institutions and homes are used and understood have been more cyclical than linear in nature, apparently reflecting the swings in political ideologies and macro-economic realities. For example, one finds a progressive international child care movement emerging after the Second World War (Courtioux, Davies Jones, Kalcher, Steinhauser, Tuggener & Waaldijk, 1985), with a resurgence in the early 1970s (Papanek, 1972) and apparently rising yet again being led by a wave of studies in the 1990s in the United Kingdom (see Department of Health, 1998). Such a cyclical developmental pattern is also notable in allied service fields such as parent education and support (Anglin, 1985).

The origin of the present European and North American systems of residential care for dealing with deviance and dependency of young people can be traced to the revolution in social practices that occurred at the end of the 18th and the beginning of the 19th centuries (Colton, 1988; Parker, 1988; Ward, 1995). Until the 20th century, there was a primary emphasis on institutional care. Large numbers of young people were housed in orphanages, industrial or training schools, hospitals for the mentally or physically disabled, and boarding schools. While there developed a movement towards foster care (the care of young people in the homes of other families) in the 19th century, the group residential care sector in Canada remained largely one of big institutions until the 1960s. At this point, an ideological groundswell of "deinstitutionalization" (after Goffman, 1961), "radical non-intervention" (Schur, 1973), and "normalization" (Wolfensberger, 1972) caught the imagination of those in the social care field, and the move to smaller, community-based homes was underway. The work of Goffman (1961) on asylums and the concept of "the total institution" along with the research on infant attachment by Bowlby (1958, 1969) were particularly influential in this regard. The contemporaneous advent of a governmental emphasis on cost-benefit analysis only added to the momentum (Schur, 1973).

In Canada, the earliest residential institutions were the orphanages founded by the Ursiline nuns in Quebec in the early 1700s. The primary emphasis was the provision of housing and basic care for the homeless, orphaned, and impoverished. For the socially deviant, the goal was segregation from mainstream society and "correction." In the 1800s, the emphasis on protection of children emerged, culminating in legislation in Canada such as the Act for the Prevention of Cruelty to and Better Protection of Children (Fewster & Garfat, 1993). Welfare organizations, usually of a religious nature, ushered in the "child saving" era which persisted until the Second World War. The 1930s and 1940s saw increased specialization in the nature of the institutions (e.g., physical and mental disabilities, delinquency, emotional disturbance, etc.) and a strong shift toward foster home care for those who needed a home and were without severe special needs (Turner, 1979).

An important and regrettable development, emerging from the initial encounters of early European colonists and the Aboriginal peoples living in the territory that became Canada, was the creation of residential schools for Aboriginal children in the 1880s (Chrisjohn & Young, 1997; Fournier & Crey, 1997; Miller, 1996). To this day, hundreds of court cases remain to be resolved concerning allegations of abuse and mistreatment of young Native children, and many horrific stories have been documented and validated in relation to residential schools across the country (Haig-Brown, 1988; Miller, 1996). While these schools were developed as the result of government policies of assimilation, most of them were run by religious orders of various denominations. The last of these institutions were not phased out until the 1960s (Miller, 1996). Since about 50% of young people in care in Canada are of Aboriginal descent, any detailed consideration of the future of residential care as a service will need to acknowledge this and take into account this history.

By the 1960s and 1970s, the specialized residential facilities in Canada and the United States were increasingly focusing on doing "treatment." Medical doctors, psychiatrists, or psychologists were hired either as institutional directors or as "treatment directors." With this movement emerged a redefinition of the role of the careworkers from custodians to "milieu therapists" (Treischman, Whittaker, & Brendtro, 1969). At the same time, most institutions were being built with a number of small cottages, generally with 12 to 20 "beds," in an effort to emulate a more "family-style" environment. One of the aims of this study is to explore the degree to which a "family-style" environment can, and should, be created by community-based group home residences.

In the early 1970s a major Canadian report on children with learning disabilities addressed the topic of residential care, and it heavily condemned both the large institutions that were still in operation in many parts of the country and the notion of treatment that they espoused:

While residential programs are necessary they are also regrettable. It is regrettable that they are necessary. . . . Residential programs are cannibalistic of scarce professional staff and by giving greater amounts of time and attention to a very small number of individuals they magnify present and future shortages. . . .

Residential treatment is prodigal rather than parsimonious of resources and therefore should be used for as few cases as possible for the briefest possible periods required to be effective. . . . Residential care and treatment are a drastic interruption of the normal pattern and environment of a child's maturation and growth. Residential treatment always compounds difficulties or creates them, particularly if there are major differences and conflicts between the values and expectations of the family and the institution. Separation from the experiences needed for normal growth and development should be as short as possible with primary emphasis on flexible child rearing programs of group home care, and the most rapid return to normal rather than highly artificial living situations. (Rae-Grant & Moffat, 1971, pp. 98-101)

In summary, the major shifts in the purposes of residential programs for children and youth have been from custodial ("warehousing") to protection and care ("greenhousing") and then to treatment, which perhaps could be referred to as "hothousing," in reference to the intensity of intervention (Barnes, 1991, pp. 123-155). Some studies undertaken during the period of evolution into the treatment era have indicated that while there may have been a rhetoric of treatment in a home, the day-to-day practice appeared to consist largely of routine care activities (e.g., Berridge, 1985). At the same time, whatever the particular purposes and functions being addressed by particular residential settings, there remains the question of determining for whom they are appropriate.

FOR WHOM IS RESIDENTIAL GROUP CARE APPROPRIATE?

Residential group care, as opposed to foster family care or adoption, has been recommended in the literature for a number of reasons. For example, Utting (Department of Health, 1991) suggests group care for children and adolescents who:

have decided that they do not wish to be fostered;
have had bad experiences in foster care;
have been so abused within the family that another family placement is inappropriate; or
are from the same family and cannot otherwise be kept together. (p. 8)

A growth in support for foster care and adoption followed the influential studies by Bowlby (1958, 1969) and Ainsworth (1972) on the importance of attachment and attachment formation in childhood. Children raised in orphanages and other large institutions were seen to be deprived of the effects of maternal nurturing that could be provided best by a mother and within a family home.

More recently, the influential Wagner (1988) report in the United Kingdom indicated that the main continuing need for residential child and youth care services is in the following situations:

1. Respite care, by providing periods of planned relief in residence, is considered of the greatest importance, enabling both natural and foster families to continue to care for their disturbed or handicapped members.
2. Preparation for permanent placement: It is evident that an increasing number of children who have experienced multiple breakdowns in previous living arrangements need a structured, caring, nurturing, but not emotionally demanding environment linked with a realistic plan for their future.
3. Keeping families together: Residential provision should be used to enable brothers and sisters to stay together.
4. Care and control: For a small minority of children identified as a risk to themselves or others, a certain amount of specialist provision is required, but it is considered important to minimize the use of secure care.
5. Therapeutic provision: For socially and emotionally damaged children therapeutic provision has an important role to play. (pp. 96-97)

Wagner's (1988) overall conclusion regarding residential group care was that "we firmly believe that there are circumstances in which group living will be the preferred choice and that the appropriate provision, which is not necessarily in the form of large establishments, needs to be made available and developed" (p. 99). An influential document entitled "Children in the Public Care: A Review of Residential Child Care," often referred to as "The Utting Report," concluded that "Residential Care is an indispensable service . . . that should be a positive, joint choice, primarily for adolescents, who may present challenging behaviour" (Department of Health, 1991, p. 62).

In the same vein, this study of residential care will observe current placement practices in a sample of homes in British Columbia and will consider whether there are characteristics of group home care that may indicate its use as a positive and even preferred alternative to foster care for at least a transitional period for some young people requiring out-of-home care. In recent years, foster care has been generally considered the placement of choice when out-of-home care is required for a young person, as there is a belief that "a family is the best place for every child" (Boone, 1999).

HOW FAR CAN OR SHOULD THE STATE SEEK
TO EMULATE THE FAMILY?

As Konopka (1970) points out, "The idea of institutions as family units had occurred because we had learned about the importance of close family life and its psychological meaning to the development of every human being" (p. 13). As noted earlier, the movement towards family-like programs was prompted in large measure by the work of John Bowlby (1958, 1969) on mother-child attachment and bonding.

Konopka (1970) further maintains that "the child or youngster knows that the institution cannot offer the same situation as a real family. . . . A child in his own family, for instance, knows that his parents are 'stuck with him' " (p. 14). The issue of continuity of care, including the effects of changed placements and turnover of staff, has been explored in-depth in the child and youth care literature over the past 20 years, and yet no matter how long social workers or child and youth care workers remain in their positions, or how few moves the child makes within the system, staff are very rarely if ever going to provide the life-long continuity characteristic of most parents or extended family members.

How do we understand families and family life in the child and youth care field, and what influences do these understandings have on the provision of residential care service? Millham et al. (1986) note that several studies, including those by Lasson (1978), Berridge (1985), Rowe and Lambert (1973), and Fanshel and Shinn (1978), have suggested that caregivers do not perceive themselves as replacement parents, and their own study corroborates these findings.

> Our study will also demonstrate that many children experience long stays in residential care which, whatever its considerable and usually unrecognised strengths, finds it difficult to replicate family life. Consequently, substitute parenting and an enduring relationship, are not easily constructed for a child. As a result, the advisability of maintaining parental and wider family contact should be self-evident. (Millham et al., 1986, p. 118)

Prosser (1976) is even more forceful in a critique of residential care as a replacement for family: "In terms of bringing up children in circumstances that approximate most nearly to those of a normal family, residential care would seem to offer the most costly and the least beneficial alternative" (Prosser, p. 25).

Leonard Davis (1987), who for many years worked as a child and youth care practitioner, teacher, and consultant, provides a description of what appears to be a common reality in his collection of articles *Rivers of Pain, Bridges of Hope*:

> I identified in a local authority children's home caring for 28 young people in four units the following hierarchy: head of home, deputy head of home, assistant head of home, four unit leaders, four deputy unit leaders, plus basic care staff (full time and part time) and students, all of whom were constantly reminded of their places in the pecking order. . . . I often wonder what the young people think of this setting as an alternative to family living, and to what extent it provides an environment for sustained personal concern, shared decision-making and the development of mutually rewarding relationships, concepts which I see as central to the work in which we are engaged. (Davis, 1987, p. 11)

While he questions the family-like nature of most residential homes, he appreciates the need for good residential work with young people by skilled and well-trained staff.

> On the one hand, I have frequently encountered what seem intractable problems, leading to emotional pain rarely found outside residential settings. On the other, it has often been possible to work towards the resolution of difficulties by building with residents bridges of hope, helping both young people and adults to find ways of managing and overcoming stress and distress. (Davis, 1987, p. 1)

The degree to which a residential home can and does fulfill family functions and nurture the emotional development of the young residents, and to what extent there is shared "parenting" with the natural families of the children, needs to be better understood.

Families typically perform the functions of procreation, socialization, provision of residence, economic support, and emotional support (Eichler, 1983, pp. 8-9). Residential programs are able to address the socialization, residential, economic, and emotional functions characteristic of family life. However, the research literature on residential care does not provide much support for the aspiration of many residential homes to be "family-like." That goal appears quite unrealistic and increasingly without clear meaning. Family life is more than fulfilling functions.

In order to better understand the issues related to the "familial" nature of group home life, the sample of homes being studied here will be examined in terms of their attempt to replicate or approximate a family atmosphere, and the experiences and perceptions of the children and youth, the home staff, and others will also be explored in this regard. In more recent North American child and youth care literature, there has been considerable debate over the degree to which the carework function in residential care does or should approximate the parenting function (see, for example, Goocher, 1996; Shealy, 1996a, 1996b; VanderVen, 1996).

RESIDENTIAL CAREWORK AS SUBSTITUTE PARENTING

The opinions of researchers and authorities in the area of residential care have varied widely on the issue of whether carework can be equated to parenting, as illustrated by the following two quotations:

> Good child care work is, basically, good parenting. Child care workers are surrogate parents. The word "surrogate" comes from the Latin "surrogatum" which means "to put in another's place." Child care workers are raising or re-raising children in the place of biological parents. (Barnes, 1986, p. 122)

> As we have acknowledged clearly and firmly, residential staff are not and cannot take the place of parents, but like care staff in boarding schools and nursing staff in hospitals they have to, or should, fulfil many of the roles and tasks which parents would do if the children were at home. (Kahan, 1994, p. 327)

It would be fair to say that it is the approach taken in the latter quotation from Kahan that appears to have the greatest level of support in the recent child and youth care literature, while the former quotation represents a position more characteristic of the earlier literature in the field from the 1950s to the 1970s.

As background to the issue of residential child and youth care workers as parents, it may be useful to consider further what we understand the term "parent" to mean. The concept "parent" has at least two main components, that of *status* (or relationship) and *function*.

Parenting as a status or relationship refers to the fact that one is *responsible* for the upbringing and care of a child or, at least, a dependent. (In this sense, one is always a parent even when one's children become adults.) In many instances, likely in most cases within most societies, this relationship involves a biological parent or parents caring for one or more of their offspring. However, in a significant number of situations, parents are responsible for children who are not their offspring. In these situations, they may have the status of parents as the result of adoption, customary Indigenous practices, assumption of legal (usually temporary) guardianship, or by some informal arrangement.

Parenting as a *functional* category refers to the fact that particular roles and tasks are performed, or are expected to be performed, by people with the status of parents. This aspect of the parent role has been emphasized to an increasing degree in recent decades in the general literature pertaining to family life as evidenced by the evolution of the word from a noun into common usage as a verb. "Parenting" is now a common shorthand for what parents do or are expected to do, and there have been numerous characterizations of what this function entails. In its simplest characterization, it entails the provision of protection, care, and nurturance. However, in modern society we have come to embellish these expectations into a much more extensive and complex set of expectations, including such aspects as identity formation, moral development, social skills acquisition, sex education, nutritional awareness, and so on (Ward, 1995).

What, then, are the implications of this for the status and functions of child and youth care workers in residential care? The evolution of terminology may be informative in this regard. In the early literature on substitute care one finds such terms as "professional houseparents" (Burmeister, 1960) and "caretakers" (Buckholdt & Gubrium, 1979) in addition to the terms "foster parents" and "staff." Recently the term "caregiver" or "carer" (as in "foster carer") has replaced "caretaker." The rather awkward term "care interactor" (Maier et al., 1995, p. 271) has been proposed as a truer representation of the complex reciprocal relationships involved in this role. It is perhaps important to add that the dominant characterization of the population of children in care has shifted from "orphans" (even when they had living biological parents) to "children with families." The emphasis on the importance of maintaining and developing links between a child in care and his or her biological parent(s) and family has increased significantly with this shift in understanding and reality (Anglin, 1984).

In brief, "residential child care" has evolved from being conceived primarily as a *substitute* activity to being understood more as a temporary and *supportive* activity in terms of families and their children (Maier, 1981, p. 59). At the same time, the status and functions of child and youth care workers have become ever more difficult to specify.

One notable attempt to identify the "roles and tasks" performed by parents that must be assumed by child and youth care workers (at least in part) when a child comes into residential care is the *Looking After Children* project (Parker, Ward, Jackson, Aldgate & Wedge, 1991; Ward, 1995). This initiative has attempted to define what these tasks are by first attempting to identify "the aims that a reasonable parent might be expected to hold for any child" (Ward, 1995, p. 16). While the overall aims may have significant commonality, there will surely be cultural differences as well. For example, Rutter (1975) observes that "parents obviously differ in the goals that they have for their children. There are well-known national, cultural and social variations in this respect" (p. 144). For example, Pugh and De'Ath (1994) note that the "growing cross-cultural literature from anthropology, sociology, and psychology points to the immense variations in child-rearing practices and beliefs" (p. 43), and the Commission on Racial Equality report (as cited in Pugh & De'Ath, 1994) emphasizes that "there is no single best way to bring up a child, and there are as many differences in childrearing practices among white and among black families as there are between them" (p. 43).

One of the aims of this study is to explore the perceptions and understandings of the various study participants in relation to their roles, including the significant roles of careworkers themselves. However, beyond the traditional "parenting" or caregiving responsibilities characteristic of residential settings, group homes are now often expected to provide "treatment" services as well.

CARE AND TREATMENT

The following definition of "treatment" was developed by the author to assist in drafting residential care standards in Ontario in the 1970s (Anglin & Working Group, 1978).

Treatment consists of:

1. attempting to bring about *directed change* in a person or persons,
2. through *individualized* attention,
3. on the basis of a guiding *theoretical framework*, and
4. a suitably comprehensive and in-depth *assessment* of the situation.

The key terms can be further clarified as follows.

1. *Directed change* means goal directed, planned, and integrated activities, supported by written recording and feedback to the goal planning activity.
2. *Individualized* attention entails the existence of a personal treatment plan, followed by personalized service delivery (even when many of the activities may be of a group nature), and regular, relatively frequent review of plans. The frequency of review will depend on the nature and intensity of the treatment program. Generally, reviews of treatment (as opposed to care) will take place at least monthly and preferably weekly.
3. A guiding *theoretical framework* can be identified as being derived from a body of legitimated knowledge (research and clinical) and will generally be informed by the experience and formal training of the workers in the program.

4. An *assessment* encompasses a review of the individual's behavior, condition, and life situation; is based upon relevant information gathered over time; includes hypotheses concerning diagnosis; and is regularly updated. The frequency of the update of the assessment will depend upon the nature and severity of the problem.

It is interesting to note that an historical review undertaken in Ontario found that in 1950, there were approximately 55 residences for "problem" children, and 5 indicated that they provided treatment. By 1978, there were approximately 825 residences, more than 650 of which claimed to provide treatment (Turner, 1979). Many of those facilities emerged from sectarian institutions whose original goals were to provide shelter, care, and training.

However, whether a residential setting is seeking to provide care or treatment, or some combination of these, a central issue pertains to the degree of quality assured in their provision.

ENSURING QUALITY CARE

Parker et al. (1991) observe that the quality of life of younger children is heavily dependent upon how they are cared for day-to-day.

A concern with more distant outcomes should not be allowed to obscure that fact. After all, it is precisely the quality of these intimate and daily experiences that are widely assumed to shape the longer-term outcomes. However, there is a dilemma because those who assume a parental role need to exercise precautionary and promotional foresight on behalf of the children for whom they are responsible. (p. 31)

The "Standards for Residential Care for Children and Youth in British Columbia" (Ministry for Children and Families, 1998) offer, apparently for the first time in Canada, a detailed set of indicators pertaining to the quality of the *experience* of children in care. However, these standards were largely based in a prior standards document from the United Kingdom (Social Services Inspectorate, 1994) and discussions of a working group consisting primarily of experienced home operators and youth in care representatives.

There have been few Canadian studies to date on the nature and functioning of residential care for children and youth. The studies by Palmer (1976) and Reichertz (1978) are notable contributions. However, these two studies are now quite dated and of questionable relevance to current societal and residential service realities. The majority of reports or commentaries on residential care are of a theoretical and statistical nature, often focused on policy development, and are not grounded in empirical research on the realities of care practice (e.g., Canadian Council on Children and Youth, 1978; Commission on Emotional and Learning Disorders in Children, 1970; Hepworth, 1975; Rae-Grant & Moffat, 1971).

The 1990s, both in Canada and the United Kingdom, have been characterized by a number of significant initiatives that have all had an impact on residential care services. These include the emphasis on quality assurance, the children's rights movement, and more open and collaborative styles of management and organization.

Quality Assurance

Much of the research on quality and quality assurance (e.g., Cassam & Gupta, 1992; Osborne, 1992; Youll & McCourt-Perring, 1993) derives its impetus from the quality management movement that has dominated the corporate and public sector thinking for the past decade. In the field of residential care for children and youth, a renewed emphasis on developing, implementing, and monitoring standards of care has been evident (Alaszewski, 1986; Storch, 1988; Zaganelli, 1988). It has reached the point that not to have an articulated set of operating standards, at the agency and government levels, is to risk being found negligent in a court of law in the event of a mishap.

However, if one examines the standards being written, one finds that there is considerable borrowing of concepts, wording, and even portions of documents by each jurisdiction from others. Further, much of what is drafted often represents some form of consensus amongst a relatively small group of workers, clinicians, and managers as to the "state of the art" of current practice. The Department of Health standards developed in the United Kingdom are notable for both their attention to empirical research and for their innovative model joining in a logical and linked progression of "outcomes for children" with "home practices" and "management actions" (Social Services Inspectorate, 1994). More empirical studies offering analyses of actual residential care practice would seem to be required as a basis for comprehensive and relevant standards development.

Children's Rights Movement

A second major influence being experienced by residential programs is the children's rights movement and the resulting principles and practices that have found their way into government policy and legislation. Well before the United Nations Convention on the Rights of the Child was proclaimed in 1989 (United Nations, 1989), government reports were acknowledging and putting forth statements of children's rights (e.g., B.C. Royal Commission on Family and Children's Law: Volume 5, 1975; Canadian Council on Children and Youth, 1978). Such developments reflected, following Fox Harding's (1991) typology introduced earlier, a predominantly protectionist orientation with a small measure of a radical perspective. Such a mix is characterized by tensions between "youth empowerment" and "state protectionism" as well as between a "legal rights" emphasis and a "child development" emphasis (Anglin, 1999).

In recent years within British Columbia and across Canada, the implementation of measures to ensure a range of children's rights in service delivery across the broad spectrum of children's programs has been given greater impetus as the result of the appointment of independent provincial officers concerned with the rights of children and youth. There are currently seven child and youth advocates in Canada, and in British Columbia, two officers report directly to the Provincial Legislature (the Ombudsman and the Child, Youth, and Family Advocate) and a third reports to the Attorney General of the province (the Children's Commissioner). However, a recent government study has resulted in a recommendation for consolidation of these offices, likely to result in one "children's officer" reporting through a Minister rather than directly to the legislature.

This groundswell of legislated concern for children's rights has begun to permeate the walls of residential facilities. Officers from both the Ombudsman's and Child Advocate's offices visit many of these settings, meet with young people in care, and distribute pamphlets to them. Larger residential agencies and service organizations involved in the drafting of practice standards typically articulate principles pertaining to the rights of children in care, often making reference to the United Nations Convention. This emphasis has sometimes drawn an anxious reaction from both parents and human service workers who are concerned that there is insufficient emphasis on children's responsibilities and on the authoritative role of adults.

Participative Organization and Management

A third force, in part an outgrowth of the feminist movement, has been the questioning of male-dominated hierarchical power structures and institutions. Discussions of women's equity, empowerment of disadvantaged groups, and "giving voice" to those on the margins (Belenky, Clinchy, Goldberger & Tarule, 1986) have added pressure for fundamental change to the traditional organizations and their functioning within society. In recent years, reflecting the desire of young people in care to also have a voice, "youth in care" groups have emerged within Canada and the United Kingdom, as well as in many other countries (see Anglin, 1992; Raychaba, 1988). While it is unclear at this time to what degree this movement has influenced the provision of direct care for young people, it is evident that workers and managers at all levels are having to respond to shifting values and perceptions regarding the empowerment of previously marginalized groups, both from within government and throughout society as a whole.

All three of these societal phenomena have also had their impact on the research enterprise, adding their influence to the growing dialogue on the nature of scientific and research paradigms and the dynamics of their creation and use (Kuhn, 1962; Lincoln & Guba, 1985; Reason & Rowan, 1981). Not only have the objects of study, in this case residential homes for children and youth, been undergoing change as a result of significant shifts in the societal cultures within which they exist, but also our understandings as researchers of the ways in which such phenomena (especially human subjects) ought to be studied and understood have also been experiencing significant challenges from "new paradigm" models (Lincoln & Guba, 1985; Reason & Rowan, 1981), and a shift from positivistic to interpretive understandings (Heshusius & Ballard, 1996; Reinharz, 1992).

In the wake of these and other transitions within contemporary British and North American society, we can no longer depend upon the findings of inquiries into residential care undertaken before the 1990s to provide adequate guidance and direction for residential practice, policy development, and research design today. Particularly in North America, the findings of empirical studies of everyday life and work within various types of residential establishments (e.g., Buckholdt & Gubrium, 1979; Palmer, 1976; Polsky, 1962; Reichertz, 1978; Trieschman, Whittaker & Brendtro, 1969) need to be tested and supplemented by more contemporary investigation.

The following chapter will introduce the specific questions that provided the impetus for the group home study and will outline the research method utilized along with a description of the research implementation process.

Chapter 2

The Staffed Group Home Study: Research Method and Implementation

Any developed theory of what counts for good practice in this [residential care] field should at least start with the hard-earned wisdom of its practitioners.

–Ian Sinclair and Ian Gibbs (1998, p. 115)

Grounded theory allows the relevant social organization and social psychological organization of the people studied to be discovered, to emerge–in their perspective!

–Barney Glaser (1992, p. 5)

BACKGROUND

The overarching questions that provided the impetus for this study were:

What is the nature of group home care and group home life for children and youth in British Columbia today?
How can group home life and work best be understood?
How congruent are the key elements, including the perceptions and experiences of constituencies in the residential care system?

Stimulated and guided in its initial stages by these broad questions, the focus of this research study became to develop a theoretical framework with which group home settings and group home life could be better understood. The ultimate purpose of such a framework is to assist in the development of standards of care, education and training initiatives, improved residential working and

[Haworth co-indexing entry note]: "The Staffed Group Home Study: Research Method and Implementation." Anglin, James P. Co-published simultaneously in *Child & Youth Services* (The Haworth Press, Inc.) Vol. 24, No. 1/2, 2002, pp. 23-48; and in: *Pain, Normality, and the Struggle for Congruence: Reinterpreting Residential Care for Children and Youth* (James P. Anglin) The Haworth Press, Inc., 2002, pp. 23-48. Single or multiple copies of this article are available for a fee from The Haworth Document Delivery Service [1-800-HAWORTH, 9:00 a.m. - 5:00 p.m. (EST). E-mail address: docdelivery@haworthpress.com].

http://www.haworthpress.com/store/product.asp?sku=J024
10.1300/J024v24n01_03

living conditions, more sensitive administrative procedures, and government policies that reflect the realities and potential of contemporary residential care practice. In brief, this study is focused primarily on *theorizing* group home life and group home work rather than on *describing* or *evaluating the effectiveness* of them. A considerable amount of descriptive data needed to be collected and analyzed, and some assessment of effectiveness needed to be made in order to construct a grounded theoretical framework.

The first step was to select a small number of staffed group homes to study in order to formulate tentative theoretical hypotheses on the basis of which further sampling could be done. While the field work involved participant observation, interviews, and review of documents, the purpose of these research activities was not to offer a description of group home life, but rather to develop a theoretical account of how group homes function. Thus this study was rooted in certain conceptions of the relationship between theory and practice that will be articulated prior to presenting and discussing the grounded theory research method that was utilized.

THE RELATIONSHIP OF THEORY AND PRACTICE

The influential social psychologist Kurt Lewin has been credited with the maxim, "There is nothing so practical as a good theory" (Hunt, 1987, p. 4). This assumption provides a basic rationale for this study of group homes. However, this maxim seems to fly in the face of the "common wisdom" in the child and youth care field. Many practitioners in the human services, including child and youth care workers, react almost viscerally in a negative way whenever theory (or anything that even sounds like theory) is presented or discussed. Those who react in such a way appear to hold a belief that the nature of child and youth care work is first and last hands-on, immediate, concrete, and practical. In contrast, theory is often thought to be by its very nature too abstract, irrelevant, generalized and therefore eminently unhelpful for such practical work with individuals in unique situations. Therefore, to maintain not only that theory can be relevant and useful, but that there is nothing *more* practical than a good theory may call for some explanation.

Lewin's provocative statement recognizes and articulates the fact that our psychosocial reality as human beings has an inherent sense of order and purpose to it. Our everyday social world is constructed by purposive action based in the meanings that objects, processes, and other persons have for us. The order within human interaction and human life is founded in the systematic organization and interrelation of such human realities as beliefs, values, ethics, thoughts, intentions, purposes, feelings, actions, behaviors, and responses.

Identifying and clarifying how these complex entities are systematically inter-connected in human experience is a task for theory building. Having an articulated theoretical framework (i.e., a systematic way of thinking) about these elements and dynamics of human action that is coherent, informative, and grounded in actual experience is to possess a powerful tool that can have very practical uses and implications for responding to concrete situations and the individual and collective actions of others.

A second basic assumption underpinning the approach adopted for this study is the converse of the first, namely: "There is nothing so theoretical as good practice" (Hunt, 1987, p. 30). What this assumption implies is that in or-der to develop a substantive theory, one must have access to instances of good practice. Thus, as will be outlined in more detail below in the section on "Initi-ating the Study," an effort was made to select primarily "well-functioning" group homes, recognizing that where the complex work of residential care is being done well, important lessons can be learned about the key elements and processes of the work and the interrelationships between them. Put another way, this approach holds that work that is consistently being done well is being done in accordance with good theoretical principles *whether or not the practi-tioners are aware of them or can articulate them*. This phenomenon is ex-plored in considerable detail by Polanyi (1958, pp. 49-65) in his explication of "tacit knowing." One everyday example illustrating this point and cited by Polanyi is that "the principle by which the cyclist keeps his balance is not gen-erally known" (Polanyi, 1958, p. 49). He goes on to outline the quite complex physical principles at play when someone achieves the balance necessary to ride a bike but of which very few bike riders are even aware.

Much of the good practice exhibited by child and youth care workers is the result of such tacit knowing. It is well known that skilled crafts people and ath-letes often cannot articulate precisely how they do what they do. It sometimes takes a less skilled but highly observant and experienced teacher or coach to be able to articulate with some precision the elements and dynamics of an expert activity or performance. "Knowing *how*" and "knowing *that*" are two different forms of knowledge (Benner, 1984, p. 2). This study is concerned with exam-ining the "know how" and tentative articulations of good practitioners as well as the experiences and perceptions of young people and their parents as a foun-dation (or the ground) for developing a theoretical framework in order to more fully understand and be able to account for the nature of residential life and res-idential child and youth care practice.

This difference in focus and purpose from more descriptive studies also leads to a major difference in the approach taken to the analysis of data. Rather than merely analyzing descriptive data for themes, the theorizing approach re-quires moving the analysis from a descriptive level to a theoretical level by "raising the data" to categories, psychosocial processes, dynamics and propositions that then form the elements of a theoretical framework (Glaser, 1978, p. 84).

There are multiple levels of theory involved in this research study. First, there are the *implicit* or tacit theoretical notions that various workers and others hold about the meaning of their work. Second, there are *explicit* formulations that guide the residential homes and that may be written down in program descriptions or may flow primarily from the directives of the home manager. Third, there are many types of *formal* theories about such phenomena as child development, child rearing, and behavior management that abound in the literature on the care and socialization of children and, most importantly in this context, have formed and shaped the minds of many residential care practitioners.

In addition, there is a fourth type of theory that constitutes the central focus of this research. This level has been referred to as *substantive* theory in recognition of its development and applicability in relation to a substantive and limited area of societal functioning (Glaser & Strauss, 1967, pp. 32-35). In this study, the substantive focus is staffed group homes for children and youth, and the goal is to articulate a theoretical framework that helps to explain how such group homes work. While a substantive framework can only claim to represent and make sense of the functioning of the entities studied, the intention is to discern the basic psychosocial processes and dynamics that would likely characterize the operation of all entities of a similar substantive nature. Of course, such a hypothesis needs to be tested and verified in further studies and applications of the framework. Indeed, one of the tests of a good substantive theory is its ability to stimulate further fruitful inquiry and research.

As was illustrated in the prior chapter, much has been written in the literature on child and youth care about many issues and policy concerns related to the provision of residential care. However, there does not as yet appear to exist, in the North American literature at least, a sufficiently well-developed or accessible theoretical framework for residential practitioners that adequately articulates the nature of successful group home care for children and youth as a service modality. Nor are there readily identifiable theoretical formulations amenable to testing or verification. This study seeks to contribute to the development of the field of group home care through the generation of a substantive theoretical framework amenable to application in practice and to serve as a guide to further investigation. The research approach adopted as most suitable for this study was "grounded theory."

THE GROUNDED THEORY METHOD

The grounded theory approach initially articulated by Barney Glaser and Anselm Strauss (1967) was selected as the most appropriate research method for the purpose of this study, namely *the development of a theoretical framework for understanding the functioning of group home work and group home life*. As has been already discussed, at the heart of the grounded theory approach is a belief in the embedded nature of theory. That is, a substantive theory of practice is implicit in good practice.

Ethical Approval and Procedures

Before initiating the study, the research study's objectives, method, procedures and ethical processes and safeguards were reviewed, as required, by the University of Victoria's Human Research Ethics Committee. The Ministry for Children and Families accepted this rigorous ethical review as sufficient and did not require any additional ethical vetting from within government. Detailed procedural guidelines based on national research standards were followed (Tri-Council, 1998), and several suggestions were made by the committee to ensure that the consent of both the young people and their guardians was obtained and was informed, that any participant could withdraw at any time without repercussions, and that the data gathered remained anonymous and secure until it was destroyed once the study was completed. Obtaining the required approvals from participants was undertaken in a step-by-step manner, beginning with an approach to the most senior manager in a prospective agency or home, followed by a meeting with and approval of home staff, and finally through obtaining the written consent of each individual interviewed. All but two of the 85 interviewees agreed to have their interviews audiotaped. Interview notes were taken in the two instances where taping did not occur.

In the event that any of the residents, former residents or other informants might disclose instances of abuse, a protocol was developed that involved informing the manager of the agency and a Ministry for Children and Families child protection worker immediately and a suspension of the researcher's involvement in the house in question pending a full review of the situation. Fortunately, this protocol did not need to be implemented over the course of the study. In addition, prior to the commencement of the study, the researcher underwent a mandatory criminal record check that is required in British Columbia for anyone working directly with young people.

The format for ensuring informed consent with participants began with a brief verbal overview of the focus of the study followed by the introduction of the consent form which also presented a written outline of the study and all relevant information about participation that every participant was asked to sign before formal involvement. Care was taken to discuss and clarify all aspects with the youth participants verbally as some had limited literacy skills.

Interview and Observation Procedures

In order to elicit the experiences, perceptions, values, beliefs, and ideas of participants in the research process with a minimum of influencing, interviews began with a general and open question that would be quite straighforward for participants to respond to, namely, "Please tell me about your background and what led you into working (or living) in (or with) this particular setting?" This initial query served to elicit some background information on the work and training of the respondents and to initiate the conversation on the basis of what they chose to present. A number of general questions were also on the researcher's interview sheet that could be used to open up conversation on various aspects of the home such as the physical house itself, program, staffing, daily living, house rules, family and community involvement, and overall satisfaction. In between these broad questions, the researcher tried to follow the informant's lead and to explore their experiences and understandings with minimal prompts (such as head nodding, requesting clarification, or asking for more information). When a topic or aspect of what was being shared appeared to have some special meaning for the informant or seemed of significance for the evolving research findings, the researcher would ask follow-up questions designed to more systematically explore those dimensions (e.g., "It seems that supervision has been particularly important in your own work; can you tell me about how you have experienced supervision in this home?" and, perhaps following this, "How does supervision affect the functioning of the staff team?" and so on). Naturally, as the research process developed over time and hypotheses were emerging within the data analysis, the exploration within the interview sessions became somewhat more focused on these dimensions while, at the same time, remaining open to unique individual perspectives and experiences of the interviewees.

The visits to the homes were largely unstructured and did not make use of observational guides in order to allow the interviewer to engage in a open manner in whatever was taking place. Visits were scheduled by the researcher to offer various "slices of life" within the homes, and to cover most of the types of activities and processes of daily life (such as wake-up time, meal times, free time periods, arriving back from school or program, family visits, staff meetings, recreation, and the like). Homes did not require advance notice; however, the researcher generally called a few minutes in advance of a visit to ensure that there were children and staff present and that there were no contagious illnesses on site. Paralleling the interview approach described above, the early stages of the visits were concerned with gaining as rich and broad an experience of life in and around the home as possible. A number of activities and meetings that occurred away from the house premises were also observed.

However, as the study progressed, the observations became somewhat more focused on processes and phenomena most relevant to the emerging constructs and hypotheses while remaining open to new experiences and events as they would occur. A summary of the hours spent on-site and the number and range of interviews is outlined in Table 1: Overview of Research Visits and Formal Interviews by Home. The detailed elements of the grounded theory research process will be introduced next within the context of the implementation of this study.

INITIATING THE STUDY

In line with Lewin's principle articulated earlier that "there is nothing so theoretical as good practice" (Hunt, 1987, p. 30), the first step in this study was to identify a sample of staffed group homes that exemplified "good practice." Homes known to be experiencing significant difficulties, in crisis, or under investigation for possible standards violations might not provide optimal opportunities to observe good practice; therefore, such homes were excluded from initial consideration. However, the need to secure a beginning sample of homes that were reasonably well-functioning presented a somewhat paradoxical challenge. While there are periodic inspections undertaken of group settings in British Columbia, these inspections are focused on monitoring a limited set of standards and do not provide an assessment of the overall level of functioning of homes.

Given that this study was intended to discover a theoretical framework that would define the elements of a well-functioning home and would be grounded in practice, it would not have been appropriate simply to apply ready-made criteria derived from existing theoretical or empirical studies. This would go against the principles of the grounded theory method and would result in a rather vicious circularity that could involve trying to "discover" in a sample of homes a set of theoretical elements that had already been used in selecting the very sample. Therefore, a set of very broad criteria was defined relating to the longevity and management stability of the homes enhancing the likelihood that the functioning of the home was a sustained rather than an ephemeral phenomenon. These broad criteria were then used in combination with the judgements of a number of experienced observers of the group homes.

In order to be a candidate for inclusion in the study sample, at least two professionals who had placed children in the home or monitored the home's operation over at least a three-year period needed to assess the potential study home to be well-functioning. The three most common characteristics mentioned by informants in relation to the homes that they suggested were the provision of

TABLE 1. Overview of Research Visits and Formal Interviews by Home

	Yellowdale	Oriole	Thunderbird	Dogwood	Pioneer Place	Parke Place	Big House	Hillside	Oak Lane	Mountain-view	Totals
Time											
Days on Site	8	6	7	5	2	6	6	2	2	6	50
Hours on Site	12.5	23.5	17	12.5	3.5	12.5	13.5	4	4.5	37	140.5
Interviews											
Number of Formal Interviews	18	9	8	5	5	10	10	2	2	16	85
Former Residents	2	0	0	1	0	3	0	0	0	2	8
Residents	2	0	2	0	0	0	1	0	0	5	10
Careworkers	3	5	2	3	1	5	6	1	0	5	31
Supervisors	1	1	2	1	1	1	1	1	0	1	9
Managers	1	-	1 (Metro)	-	1	-	1 (Valley)	-	2	1	7
Parents/ Couples	2	1	0	0	0	0	0	0	0	1	4
MCF*/ Aboriginal Agency	4	1	1	0	2	1	0	0	0	2	11
Collaterals	3	1	0	0	0	0	1	0	0	0	5

*MCF = Ministry for Children and Families

good care and a nurturing environment overall, competent staff with effective supervision, and the achievement of good outcomes for children. Naturally, these judgements were based upon the subjective assessments of the professional informants and no predetermined criteria were offered by the researcher. However, the informants all had many years of involvement with residential programs in various capacities such as resource managers, contract managers, and child placement workers. Given that any complex program takes some time to develop and mature in order to be sustainable, only homes where the leadership (i.e., the home manager) had been in place for at least four years were included.

THEORETICAL SAMPLING

Grounded theory inquiry utilizes an approach referred to as theoretical sampling (Glaser, 1978, pp. 36-44). This approach differs from random sampling, which attempts to eliminate bias through ensuring that all members of the population of interest have an equal opportunity to be included. It also differs from a selective sampling procedure, which involves defining a predetermined set of sites, locations, categories, or groups for study and analysis before the study begins. Theoretical sampling refers to the process of choosing the sample on an incremental basis over the course of the study in light of the emerging concepts, hypotheses, and theoretical formulations as the data gathering and analysis progresses. As a result, in this study of group residences neither the precise sample of homes nor the detailed elements of the settings to be examined could be determined in advance of initiating the research process.

Therefore, the study necessarily began with a selective sample in its initial phase. Then, after a period of several months, additional homes were added in order to enable systematic comparisons of data emerging from the initial observations, interviews, and analyses. This initial stage of the research will be referred to as Phase One of the study.

PHASE ONE: THE INITIAL SAMPLE

The study began with a small selective sample chosen from the approximately 500 residential group programs involving over 1,500 young people in care funded by the (then) Ministry of Social Services in the province of British Columbia (Ministry of Social Services, 1995). All but one of the homes were within the "family and child service" ("child protection") division of the Ministry. Young people, generally between the ages of 10 and 17, were placed in these settings either on a voluntary basis or as a result of being removed by the courts for alleged abuse or neglect in their previous homes. Not included in this sample were "community living" homes for young people with physical or mental challenges or mental health treatment facilities.

The Phase One sample consisted of four group homes chosen to provide diversity in terms of purpose (e.g., receiving and assessment, long-term care, intensive care), geographical location (e.g., urban and rural), and auspices (voluntary board or for-profit proprietorship). In British Columbia, the large majority of care services, including residential homes for young people, are not operated directly by the government but are contracted out through private (voluntary) agencies or "for profit" proprietors. While no precise information was available on the percentage of homes province-wide that were unionized or non-unionized, there were substantial numbers in both categories. The balance estimated by some Ministry staff members at the time of this study was about one-half in each category.

Of the first four homes selected, three were in a large urban center and one was in a semi-rural northern community. The three urban homes were in the same city and were operated by one agency that was a non-unionized proprietorship. The names of the programs have been changed to respect confidentiality and the privacy of the residents, staff members, and agencies. The initial sample included the three single-agency homes–Oriole, Thunderbird, and Dogwood–and the rural stand-alone home–Yellowdale.

Oriole was a short-term receiving home for young people from 2 years of age to 17, with four "beds" and stays of up to 90 days. A receiving home is generally used as a transitional placement in a crisis situation. Thunderbird was a longer term, four-bed home with stays of up to two years or more for teenage boys. Dogwood was an intensive care resource for 4 very challenging adolescents with multiple problems who stayed from 6 months to more than 1 year. While Thunderbird accepted only male residents, Oriole and Dogwood took both male and female youth. Each of the three homes was in a separate residential neighborhood within the city. The agency encompassing these three homes will be referred to as "Metro Agency."

The fourth home in the initial sample, Yellowdale, was located about a forty-five minute drive and almost equidistant from two medium-sized urban centers. The house accommodated 4 young boys between 10 and 14 years old and was on a rural road with large lots and homes separated by big trees.

Oak Lane, a fifth home located in a different urban area from Metro Agency, received two initial visits, but due to a change of house managers that occurred during this time, the new manager decided to delay participation in the study. However, in Phase Two of the study, interviews were held with two former managers of Oak Lane in order to explore several emerging core categories. Despite a history of over 30 years as a residential home, Oak Lane was closed over the course of this study, apparently for a combination of cost-saving reasons and a preference for more family-based services on the part of the regional governmental contracting and funding authorities.

Contacting the Homes

In order to identify the initial homes, an e-mail notice was sent to regional resource managers in the Ministry for Children and Families throughout the province providing an overview of the study and indicating that the researcher wanted to involve "well-functioning" staffed group homes from various parts of the province. Also, the Executive Director of the Federation of Child and Family Services of British Columbia, a province-wide network of agencies with residential and non-residential services, was asked to suggest homes that she knew from direct experience appeared to fit the general criterion of being well-functioning.

One resource manager from a northern area contacted the researcher and suggested a group home in his community that he assessed to be one of the best that he had encountered in over 30 years of professional work. The Federation of Child and Family Service's Executive Director also proposed six agencies that she knew had long-standing group home programs that seemed to be well-managed and appropriately supervised. After confirming these initial reports with other informed contacts both within and outside the Ministry for Children and Families at the local level, the decision was made to contact the managers of the five homes described above. Oak Lane was already somewhat familiar to the researcher while the remaining four were not.

Preliminary discussions took place by telephone followed by face-to-face meetings with the manager, program supervisors, and some of the group home staff from Oak Lane, Yellowdale, and the Metro Agency. At both Yellowdale and Oak Lane, small stand-alone homes, the manager also served as the home supervisor. The Metro Agency had one manager overseeing the agency's three homes as well as a different supervisor designated for each individual home. A one-page overview of the research project was faxed to each manager in advance to allow for some review and discussion within the agency before the meeting. The researcher then met with staff and/or supervisors from each home, briefly presented the intent and anticipated time-frame for the study, the activities to be undertaken within the research process, and answered any questions that were raised. From the start, all three agencies responded very positively and all consulted staff members expressed interest in the aims of the study. It was suggested that each group discuss the proposal after the meeting and get back to the researcher if they were willing to participate. The managers and supervisors of all five homes responded with enthusiasm and agreed to take part.

Visiting the First Four Homes

As has been indicated, early in the process the Oak Lane home underwent a change of manager and was closed shortly thereafter during the course of the study. Each of the remaining four homes was visited two or three times over the initial 2 month period. Typically, the researcher would notify the home supervisor of a planned visit in advance, and visit times were purposely varied to allow for on-site exposure to different aspects of the daily and weekly activities as well as different staff members. Early morning wake-up and breakfast times, dinner times and evenings, and weekend afternoons and evenings proved to be the most fruitful occasions as the residents tended to be either asleep or out of the homes during most of the remaining hours. Also, the researcher joined in on some of the recreational outings, court appearances, agency gatherings (such as a Christmas party), and school events in order to experience some of the engagements of residents in aspects of their broader community life.

Site visits continued over a 6-month period, generally on a monthly basis for between 2 to 4 hours per visit. In addition, group home staff, Ministry workers, former residents, and collateral contacts were interviewed, often off-site or when children were otherwise occupied in order to allow for privacy and to minimize distractions and interruptions.

As the method utilized involved ongoing analysis of data derived from on-site observations, interviews, and available documents as the basis for subsequent data gathering activities, a considerable amount of detailed analysis was done between each visit, whenever possible. Relevant documents reviewed included statements of purpose or philosophy, mission statements, program descriptions, behavioral charting guidelines, log books, case files, case plans, critical incident reports, staff schedules, and house rules. Usually these reviews were done in the staff offices when the youth were at home and interacting with staff members, and thus the researcher could experience both staff conversations away from the residents as well as "boundary" encounters at the doorway of the office.

Once the initial sample of four homes had been engaged over the initial eight-month period, it was necessary to expand the sample to include more homes in order to explore further, and in different contexts, some of the emerging categories, psychosocial processes, and hypotheses concerning the dynamics of home functioning. The approach followed in order to engage five more staffed residences will be outlined in the next section.

It is important to note here that the theoretical sampling procedure was not just relevant for the selection of sites but was also important in the process of data collection within sites. While the observation process began without any predetermined scope in order to allow the researcher to be exposed to as many aspects of the homes as possible, gradually the timing of visits and selection of activities to observe became more targeted.

For example, in the first home that was engaged, Yellowdale, virtually everyone involved with the home was interviewed and recorded on audio tape, and all of the tapes were transcribed and analyzed. In subsequent homes, the interviews became increasingly more selective, and the tapes analyzed without typing out full transcripts. Only selected portions of the tapes were transcribed, and the analysis of tapes gradually shifted from an emphasis on descriptive labels (e.g., "staff and youth harvesting wood") to formulating theoretical categories (e.g., "doing *with*, rather than doing *to*"). This technique reflected the purpose of the analysis, namely, the raising of data to the level of theoretical constructs and, therefore, there was no need for verbatim transcription and line-by-line analysis of every data element as the research progressed. In addition, field observations were, for the most part, written up immediately after a period of immersion in the home (generally 2-4 hours in duration), and these notes (termed "memos") were also reviewed alongside the interview data.

Access to the homes was a critically important issue. Most of the homes extended an open invitation to the researcher to visit at any time without advance notice, and many of the visits were made immediately after a courtesy call without prior scheduling. Visits were postponed in only a few instances due to an absence of youth on site or because of a contagious illness in the home.

PHASE TWO: EXTENDING THE SAMPLE

While all of the first four homes making up Phase One of the sample met the general selection criterion for being deemed "well-functioning," the decision was made to include two of the Phase Two homes even though they did not currently meet this criterion. On the basis of the experience in this study, perhaps a third principle could be added to Kurt Lewin's initial two regarding the relationship of theory and practice: "There is nothing like poor practice to put good practice into perspective." Contrasts between the better functioning and less well-functioning homes highlighted and reinforced many of the emerging elements, processes, and dynamics gaining the attention of the researcher.

As has already been discussed, the theoretical sampling method is an integral aspect of the grounded theory approach that requires the researcher to make a number of important decisions as the research study evolves that cannot be prescribed in advance. These decisions include such aspects as,

    a. whether to continue with examination of the existing sites or not and, if
       so, in what respects;
    b. how to extend or broaden the sample and along which dimensions;
    c. what research strategies to use, such as observation, interviews, or document review; and
    d. what the particular focus or foci of the next phase of data gathering activities will be.

A number of the preliminary findings from the first four homes influenced the selection of subsequent sites.

First, the early experiences with the Metro Agency suggested that a clustering of residential programs within one organization could offer important advantages (such as more flexible staffing patterns, better matching of staff to homes, and enhanced administrative capacity and support), and the involvement of a second agency with a clustering of residential homes was considered to be desirable for comparative purposes. In addition, it would assist in the comparative analysis to include such an agency from a different region of the province, perhaps with a unionized staff and voluntary board governance structure, given that Metro Agency was a non-unionized proprietorship. Such diversity would allow for further exploration of the relationships between some of the structural factors and the nature and quality of the carework, supervision, and management processes being discovered.

With the assistance of the Executive Director of the provincial Federation of Child and Family Services Association, the "Valley Agency" was identified. The Valley Agency, situated in a smaller urban center in the interior of the province, proved to be an ideal choice. As with the Metro Agency, it also ran multiple programs: the Parke Street receiving home, a brief stay (four days) youth shelter (the Big House), and Hillside, a three bed long-term resource that had the added advantage of being a mixed staff and parent model. In addition, many of the staff in these three residences had also worked in a long-term home that had been closed recently by the Valley Agency. As a consequence, staff members were able to speak to their experiences across a broader range of residential work than the three participating homes alone. The home that had been recently closed had some similarities to the Metro Agency's Thunderbird home, while Parke Street was designed to serve a similar "receiving and assessment" purpose as was the Oriole home. At the same time, Hillside and the Big House offered some unusual and new features to the sample.

The Hillside home was created for three young boys requiring very intensive care and supervision. The houseparents were a young couple with their own baby, supported by child and youth care staff in the home for about 24 hours a week to allow the parents some "down time." An unusual feature of this arrangement was the fact that this home was considered the boy's home, and if the houseparents decided to end the arrangement, the boys would stay in the home and new parents would be recruited to live in the home.

The opportunity to examine a residential home that bordered on a foster care approach seemed promising and timely. One of the questions in the minds of many Ministry and collateral interviewees in the initial sample that had become evident to the researcher was how to determine when it was appropriate to place a child in residential care rather than in foster care. There was a belief amongst some placement workers that residential care was highly intrusive and always less desirable as a care setting than foster care. There were also pressures evident from senior Ministry management to significantly reduce the use of group home placements in favor of regular or specialized foster care. The Ministry had developed a classification system that identified three levels of specialized foster care that were defined in accordance with the type of foster parent qualifications and the amount of therapeutic and special supports required by the child being placed, and the foster homes were accordingly differentially funded. Level Three was the most intensive of the three levels, and Level One was the least intensive, with all three being funded at a higher rate than "regular" foster care. Hillside was classified as a Level Three home.

The issue of the place of group homes on the continuum of care resources also raised issues about the nature of institutionalization. During the course of this study, and in relation to the closure of a group home, the Minister for Children and Families had stated publicly that the Ministry was moving away from "institutional care" for children, clearly implying that a group home was an institution (Boone, 1999). This public statement added a sense of urgency to the researcher's growing interest in the process of institutionalization, and the inclusion of Mountainview, a youth residential setting with a correctional focus and fourteen beds, appeared to offer an excellent opportunity to further examine this phenomenon.

Fortuitously, the Mountainview residential resource had been suggested for the study, as it had a national reputation for excellence and effectiveness without the usual bureaucratic trappings of correctional institutions. It was also apparent that such a program would allow for a close look at the influence of a fundamentally different philosophy (namely, a correctional as opposed to a child welfare approach) on the carework, supervision, and management processes being identified in the initial sample. Over the course of the study, it became evident that the staff members at Mountainview had succeeded in creating a rather unique blend of correctional and child welfare approaches.

Traditionally, there has been some philosophical tension evidenced within the child and youth care field between a child welfare orientation and a juvenile or youth corrections approach (Fewster & Garfat, 1993; Philips & Maslowsky, 1993). The (then) newly formed Ministry for Children and Families, bringing together these two approaches into one government body for the first time in the province, had not yet addressed this issue in any concerted manner. It was evident that involving this correctional residence could inform the evolving framework and hypotheses of this research study on both the philosophical and institutional dimensions.

Further, the Mountainview residence was located in a northern and rural part of the province that would allow for more consideration of the impact of regional differences. Mountainview operated a wilderness trip component and it accepted groups of 7 male youth for 4 months at a time, overlapping two groups at 2 month intervals. The outstanding reputation of this residential program proved to be well-founded, and it offered an extremely fruitful source of data on the functioning of staffed residential care as well as for some analysis of the functioning of a larger group care setting that was striving to avoid becoming significantly institutionalized or bureaucratic.

The final group home selected, Pioneer Place, was located in a forested area about fifteen kilometers outside of a mid-size urban center and was a residence for up to 8 male adolescent sexual offenders. This home was visited by the researcher on only two occasions, as some of the staff were reluctant to have the researcher observe while they were on shift. However, one staff member, two therapists, the program manager, and a former supervisor were interviewed off the premises and provided much valuable information about residential group home work in general as well as specific to working with a population of residents with some unique and intensive service demands.

Expanding the sample in this manner also offered an opportunity to undertake a different home-visiting pattern than had been followed in Phase One. This opportunity was in part prompted by logistical convenience, due to the large geographical distances necessitating travel by air, and in part born of research curiosity. As the research evolved, the researcher had become increasingly interested in the question of whether a more intensive and concentrated involvement in the daily life of the homes would reveal different aspects or different levels of depth than the "dipping in and out" pattern of the first phase of the study.

Therefore, for Mountainview and the three Valley Agency settings it was decided to spend 2 one-week periods, about a month apart, in each of the two geographical locations. This allowed for a similar number of site visits and interviews to be made as were made with the initial sample group and for the researcher to experience the patterns and flow of residential activity over more intensive and abbreviated periods of time. Table 2 provides a profile of all ten residences involved in this study and compares them across some of the major structural and resident dimensions.

THE EMERGENCE OF THEORY

While the grounded theory approach is primarily an inductive method, deductive processes play a significant role. In this study, the initial emerging theoretical contructs and tentative hypotheses concerning group home life and work were developed inductively on the basis of the analysis of early data, while questions and directions for further elaboration were, in turn, deduced from the emerging theoretical propositions. However, this deductive analysis was made in service of the primarily inductive method, and hypotheses so derived were continually assessed in relation to the research data. As a result,

TABLE 2. Profile of Group Residences in Study

Name	Size	Length of Stay	Location	Auspices	Residents
Yellowdale	4 beds	6-18 months	semi-rural	proprietorship (non-union)	male, 10-14 years
Oriole*	4 beds	up to 90 days	large urban	proprietorship (non-union)	female and male, 10-17
Thunderbird*	4 beds	6 months-2+ years	large urban	proprietorship (non-union)	male, 10-17
Dogwood*	4 beds	6 months to 1+ years	large urban	proprietorship (non-union)	female and male, 13-17
Pioneer Place*	8 beds	1-2 years	rural	society & board (union)	male, 13-18
Parke St.**	5 beds	6 months-1+ years	small urban	society & board (union)	female and male, 12-17
Big House**	5 beds	4 days	small urban	society & board (union)	female and male, 14-17
Hillside**	3 beds	indefinite and long term	small urban	society & board (union)	male, 12-16
Oak Lane	5 beds	6 months to 2 years	large urban	society & board (non-union)	male, 9-11
Mountain-view	14 beds	4 months	wilderness	society & board (non-union)	male, 14-17

*Metro Agency Homes
**Valley Agency Homes

many were discarded or put aside as too peripheral to a core theoretical understanding.

The grounded theory method requires that the researcher take time out from data gathering on a regular basis in order to code and analyze before the amount of data gathered becomes overwhelming. While it would perhaps have been ideal in this study if the coding and analysis of all of the data could have be done following each group home visit or interview, on a number of occasions the demands of scheduling and transcription of tapes entailed a review of the notes and tapes from several visits and interviews at one time.

For example, on several occasions two or three homes were visited intensively over several days, and the short time between visits meant that coding of observations and interviews had to be undertaken a few days later. This was especially true in Phase Two of the study when frequent visits were undertaken to the three Valley Agency sites within two one-week periods. In this situation, the researcher would allocate a period of time, preferably a full day, after every day or two of data gathering in order to review the materials and to undertake an intense period of coding in advance of the next visit. While such periods involved intensive concentration for long hours, these times of immersion in the data from several settings proved very conducive to the process of theoretical coding that was required.

THEORETICAL CODING

In the grounded theory method, the process of coding is different from the approach taken in descriptive studies. Whereas in descriptive studies the coding attempts to categorize and label the descriptive elements, in the grounded theory approach these descriptive codes must then be raised to the status of theoretical codes (Glaser, 1978, pp. 6-7).

While various terms can be used for the different levels of codes, in this study the term "construct" was used for the lower-level descriptive codes and the term "category" used for the broader or higher level codes. "Core categories" are those theoretical categories that prove to be central to the final formulation of the explanatory theoretical framework. In order to illustrate the theoretical aspects of the coding process undertaken in this study, a specific example will be offered.

In Phase One of the study, after numerous site visits and interviews across four settings, the following memo was written that summed up a significant portion of the data and raised them to the level of a theoretical category:

May 8, 1999:

There is a form of congruence that permeates the language of Yellowdale home; the supervisor/head, the staff, the Ministry contacts, and the children themselves. Further, the congruence appears to relate quite closely to the Head's "way of knowing" (see Artz's book for key words and phrases?).

My initial impression of the Head of Yellowdale Home, from the very first discussion, was of a very thoughtful person with a primarily cognitive approach to understanding and addressing behavior change. However, it was not until I reviewed the transcripts as a block that I was struck by the degree of consistency across the various sectors of informants (head, home staff, ministry officials, residents, ex-residents, collaterals) in reflecting this "cognitive" approach to making sense of the program and the process of change which characterizes it.

Without having yet undertaken a systematic analysis of the interviews from the other three homes with this category in mind, it is my impression that there will indeed be some noticeable differences between homes and some similar consistency across the various sectors of persons involved with each home. . . .

If the type of pattern observed in Yellowdale is evident in other homes, the related research and theory [on ways of knowing] will need to be more fully explored and articulated as background to the analysis.

As the analysis progressed and this hypothesis concerning the potential significance of "congruence" was further explored, a template was created that distinguished between four "ways of knowing" or learning styles (i.e., sensing, thinking, feeling and intuiting modes). These constructs derived initially from the work of Carl Jung but were summarized in a readily accessible form in a book by Artz (1994). The formulations provided by Artz were analyzed for key terms that served to differentiate the four ways of knowing. When the interviews that had been completed in the first four homes were analyzed through this "ways of knowing lens," a high degree of consistency in the terms and constructs used by informants was observed across interviews within each home. Furthermore, different dominant patterns were evident within each of the various homes.

Thus this procedure began the process of confirming the notion of "congruence" as a significant category relatively early on in the analysis. As the conversations and transcripts were analyzed, what came to be termed the "flow of congruence" became more clearly evident from the head/manager down the hierarchy of levels, or domains, all the way to the young residents and former residents themselves. (This notion will be explored in some detail in Chapter 4.)

It is important to note here that the use of Jung's typology was not "laid on" the data prior to discovering the category of congruence. Quite to the contrary, the notion of congruence presented itself first, and the typology was merely used to ensure that there was indeed a discernible pattern in the data that could be verified beyond the initial impressionistic perceptions of the researcher. Also, in the last analysis it was not Jung's typology or even the notion of "ways of knowing" that was most significant for this study. Rather, it was the notion of congruence itself, transcending any particular means of tracing, analyzing or verifying it.

In fact, even though this particular analysis of "congruence" within the individual homes was undertaken fairly early on in the study, it was put aside several times as other categories emerged, such as "pain and pain-based behavior" and "a sense of normality." These emerging categories each drew the researcher's attention as strong candidates for the status of "core categories." As will be explored in some detail in Chapter 5, the notion of "congruence" proved to be the most pervasive and integrative of all of the major categories and therefore emerged as the single most unifying category in the framework. The other major categories, while significant, were relegated to sub-core category status.

Thus, in the grounded theory approach the direction for future data gathering is continually shaped and guided by just such analytic processes. These processes, generally referred to collectively as the "constant comparative method" (Glaser & Strauss, 1967, pp. 21-22), represent a significant divergence from some other approaches to collecting data where the bulk of the data is gathered prior to any significant analysis being undertaken. This approach is in further contrast to methods that approach the data with preconceived categories into which to fit the data. Such preconceptions assume the relevance and significance of certain processes and elements, usually derived from previous theoretical formulations or study findings. While this may mean that the grounded theorist spends somewhat longer in the field developing the data analysis categories, the momentum of idea generation and theory development is sustained by the coding, analysis, and memoing.

MEMOING

Memoing refers to the process of writing notes documenting the conceptual and theoretical insights that happen as the researcher compiles and analyzes the data. The memoing process proved to be an important element of this study, as it was the memos that both guided the discovery process and suggested ways of raising the data and categories beyond "full description" to the status of theoretical formulations (Glaser, 1978, p. 84). The memos themselves were sorted and resorted on a continuous basis in order to explore possible linkages and to discover relationships between and within the emerging ideas. The memo relating to the category of congruence excerpted in the previous section offers one example of the memoing process in which ideas in progress are captured in writing for future review and further reflection.

CYCLING THROUGH THE DATA

It is now evident from what has been presented that the ongoing process of coding, memoing, and re-coding (i.e., the process of constant comparison) cycles on throughout a grounded theory study until a very small number of categories emerge that appear to articulate and explain the central aspects of the phenomenon being examined. As will be seen when the theoretical framework that emerged from this study is presented in the following chapter, the notions of "congruence," "extrafamilial living environment," "pain and pain-based behavior" and "a sense of normality" emerged after an extensive analytical cycling process.

The general sequence of activities in the constant comparative analysis technique characteristic of grounded theory begins with the comparison of incident to incident with the purpose of uncovering both uniformity and variance. The term "incident" refers to any occurrence or activity observed or experienced in the field work and documented in field notes or transcripts. As these incidents were coded or labeled, the emerging concepts (i.e., ideas about the incidents such as "ways of knowing" and "consistency" mentioned in the example explored earlier in this chapter) were then assessed in relation to more incidents, thereby generating theoretical properties of the concepts and yet more hypotheses about them.

Lastly, each category (i.e., a concept that appeared to have considerable integrating and explanatory power) was compared to other major emerging categories (e.g., "congruence" with "responding to pain" and "developing a sense of normality") with the purpose of determining those that could most usefully be linked together to form the basis of a theoretical framework.

FROM EMERGENCE TO SATURATION

While it is useful and important to compare the findings of a grounded theory study with other studies in the same substantive area, it is vital in the grounded theory method, particularly as articulated by Glaser (1992), to approach the data initially in as open a manner as possible. Being "open to the data" refers to allowing for the emergence of further significant meaning and to paying close attention to the evidence in the data themselves until the concept is "saturated" (Glaser, 1978, p. 95). A concept is said to be "saturated" when, after gathering or analyzing much further relevant data, no new meanings or properties of the concept are discovered. In this study, the findings of Phase Two extended and filled out an understanding of the categories that had emerged from Phase One and, as will be articulated in the next chapter, by the completion of Phase Two, a core theme, three major psychosocial processes, five levels of group home operation, and eleven key interactional dynamics were seen to encompass the central concerns of all of the participants within group home life and work across all ten settings.

Before beginning a grounded theory study, the researcher is tempted to ask: "But what if nothing emerges from the data?" The simple answer, based upon the experience of this study and the extensive experience of other studies utilizing the grounded theory method, is that "it always does" (Glaser, 1978, p. 95). The constant comparison technique ensures that concepts and categories are generated and that, over time, certain categories come to be seen as increasingly significant in the understanding of the social processes or phenomena being studied.

Glaser (1978, p. 57) has suggested a sequence of three key questions that were used frequently throughout this study to guide the process of open coding in order to ensure its most effective use.

The first question is "What is this data a study of?" It is not an uncommon experience for the grounded theory researcher to discover that the specific problem he or she thought was to be studied is not, in fact, what emerges as important or central to understanding the area being studied. In this study, group home life and work remained central throughout the research process.

Second, "What category does this incident indicate?" Stated more fully, this step involved identifying the particular category, or property of a category, or aspect of a theoretical formulation that the particular event, behavior, or statement indicated. This question forced the researcher to generate concepts that related to other concepts (e.g., "consistency," "reciprocity," and "coherence" in relation to "congruence"), and, thus, as the major categories, their properties, and their interrelations became more clearly articulated, this question became increasingly easier to answer.

Last, the researcher asked, "What is actually happening in the data?" Stated somewhat differently: "What is the basic personal, social, or interpersonal process that makes life viable or problematic in this situation?" As has been illustrated in previous sections, throughout this exploratory, self-challenging, and data-challenging process, several major categories having the greatest and most central explanatory power emerged that transcended the particular experiences within the homes and were able to raise the data to the level of ideas necessary for theoretical understanding.

THE PROCESS OF DISCOVERY

In addition to the above questions, the coding process also required the researcher to analyze the data gathered in the group homes and from the interviews line by line, analyzing each sentence of the field notes or transcripts. This process, though extremely time consuming, ensured that the researcher was deeply immersed and fully conversant with the data. The whole analytic process was one of discovery–a "quest for meaning"–that had both a holistic and emergent nature to it. While the process of analysis was the most exhausting and often frustrating aspect of the method, it was also the most exhilarating and rewarding when concepts came together and "clicked" into core categories, propositions, and an overall theoretical framework through their relevance, fit and integrativeness.

At the same time, there were many weeks when little progress appeared to be being made, with corresponding fears that the seemingly countless hours might prove to be fruitless in the end. However, after a very intensive series of observations across several homes in Phase Two of the study, accompanied by intensive hours of analysis, it was as if the dam broke. At this point, the core categories seemed to coalesce and cohere into an irreducible and rather elegant (i.e., simple yet integrative) framework. And even though numerous attempts were made to eliminate or collapse two or more of the categories, only minor refinements could be made in light of the data, and the remaining categories were all confirmed as essential to the final framework. This process of analysis and formulation reaffirmed in the researcher's mind the importance of what Glaser calls "theoretical sensitivity" (Glaser, 1978).

THEORETICAL SENSITIVITY

Theoretical sensitivity refers to what a researcher brings to the analytic aspect of the grounded theory inquiry (Glaser, 1978, p. 1). While it is true that concepts and categories have an emergent quality and that due to the inherent theoretical nature of socially constructed reality one can be said to *discover* theory, in the end the whole process perhaps can most accurately be described as *co-creative*: the coming together of an inherent and preexisting rationality implicit in the social order as the researcher examines it, with the creative and informed analytical skill and insight of the researcher.

In the group home study, while the theoretical memos became the fund or "storage bank" for the resulting theoretical framework, it was the sorting and analyzing processes that proved key to formulating the theoretical framework and in constructing the written account. It became evident to the researcher that while theory may emerge, it cannot write itself. The sorting process puts the fragmented or fractured data back together through the organizing of the ideas generated out of the data. For example, many separate words and phrases are given new meaning by the formulation of the notion of "congruence," and the notion of "congruence" thereby remains grounded in the data. Thus, the theoretical integration process began in the form of an outline of general categories generated by theoretical sorting. The outline, rather than being preconceived, emerged from the sorting of the categories and properties in the memos, and thus resulted from a creative–but always grounded–process. The initial stages of sorting in this study involved reviewing the set of constructs and categories that had emerged over the course of the data collection and analysis and attempting to cluster them on a large piece of cardboard in the form of a "concept map." This graphic exercise proved invaluable to the success of the final, integrative stages of framework construction.

Openness to emergence, one of the key tenets of grounded theory development that is shared with ethnographic research in general, is articulated by Alasuutari (1995):

> As Malinowski stressed, it is particularly important . . . to approach your object of study with an open mind and on its own terms, that during the stage of fieldwork you forget all theories and hypotheses. In practice this is of course impossible, but what Malinowski probably meant here was that you have to make observations about everything that is observable, not just about things whose utility can be deduced from the theory you have. The more open-minded you are in gathering observations, the less you exclude, the richer your material will be, and, accordingly, the better your chances of inventing completely new (theoretical) ideas on the basis of the material. (pp. 165-166)

The central concept of "emergence" needs to be understood in this context as being the opposite of a process that can be characterized as "forcing" (Glaser, 1992, pp. 3-4, 15). Forcing occurs when data are fit into a preexisting framework, while a process of emergence occurs when a framework is discovered within the data themselves. Thus, when using grounded theory, the researcher is more the discoverer of theory than the originator of theory, although the researcher's particular articulation of the integrating theoretical framework will depend upon the researcher's own theoretical sensitivity. In this sense, the process can be understood as "co-creative." Embedded within reality are multiple, if not infinite, unarticulated theories.

Alasuutari concludes his discussion of open-mindedness by reminding us that it is not the same as empty-headedness: "The paradox here is that one of the best ways to teach yourself that crucial skill of open-mindedness is to read and study as many different theories as possible" (Alasuutari, 1995, p. 166).

It is one of the hallmarks of grounded theory that it attempts to uncover categories and theoretical formulations that may not have been previously identified and articulated in the literature or by the researcher, and it has achieved demonstrated success in this task in a wide range of studies (Glaser, 1993, 1994). In this study, the theoretical framework that emerged will be seen to offer some new insights as well as confirmation and an integration of a number of quite well-established concepts and propositions.

THEORETICAL INTEGRATION

Theoretical integration, the process of pulling together the ideas generated in memos and theoretical codes into a coherent framework, ought to reflect the patterns inherent in the social reality being studied. In Glaser's words, "Grounded ideas will integrate because reality is integrated" (1978, p. 118). The assumption being made is that the social organization of the world is necessarily and inherently integrated, and the job of grounded theory is simply to discover this pattern. In the group home study, key psychosocial patterns were discovered as a result of constant comparison and through the use of concept mapping. After a number of cycles through the data and the emergent categories, a succinct one-page visual representation of the overall draft theoretical framework was created, and the final form of this graphic will be included in the following chapter outlining the key elements of the framework.

SUMMARY

The grounded theory approach is a systematic attempt to discover or uncover the intrinsic patterns and relations embedded within the domains of everyday human and social life. Hence, the word "discovery" in the book title *The Discovery of Grounded Theory* (Glaser & Strauss, 1967) refers to the process of finding theory in the world that occurs in each study rather than to the discovery or invention of the method itself.

The development of theory is a neverending process, and this study seeks to contribute to the evolution of theory in the area of residential care and residential life for young people. The grounded theory method is based on a belief that social life is inherently meaningful and ordered to the participants living it, and, therefore, the task of grounded theory research is to allow this meaning and order to emerge from the process of engaging with the persons-in-context and their reality in an intensive and systematic manner.

Table 2 provides an overview of the number of visits, hours on site, and formal interviews broken down by home and category of respondent.

The next chapter will provide a brief outline of the major elements of the theoretical framework that emerged from this research study on staffed group homes.

Chapter 3
A Theoretical Framework for Understanding Group Home Life and Work

What is distinguishable theoretically is not necessarily separable in fact: for to distinguish elements in a whole theoretically is merely to limit attention to an aspect of what is presented.

–John MacMurray (1957, p. 128)

The purpose of this study was to construct a theoretical framework that would offer an understanding of staffed group homes for young people that, in turn, could serve as a basis for improved practice, policy development, education and training, research, and evaluation. The method selected as most appropriate to the task of developing a theoretical understanding of group home life and work was the grounded theory method as articulated in a variety of texts by the co-founders of the method, Barney Glaser and Anselm Strauss (Glaser, 1978, 1992; Glaser & Strauss, 1967; Strauss, 1987; Strauss & Corbin, 1990). The development of grounded theory was influenced by the emerging tradition of "symbolic interactionism" (Blumer, 1969; Strauss & Corbin, 1990, p. 24). The central tenets of symbolic interactionism are perhaps most succinctly conveyed in Blumer's own words:

> Symbolic interactionism rests in the last analysis on three simple premises. The first premise is that human beings act toward things on the basis of the meanings that the things have for them. . . . The second premise is that the meaning of such things is derived from, or arises out of, the social interaction that one has with one's fellows. The third premise is that these meanings are handled in, and modified through, an interpretative process used by the person in dealing with the things he encounters. (Blumer, 1969, p. 2)

[Haworth co-indexing entry note]: "A Theoretical Framework for Understanding Group Home Life and Work." Anglin, James P. Co-published simultaneously in *Child & Youth Services* (The Haworth Press, Inc.) Vol. 24, No. 1/2, 2002, pp. 49-59; and: *Pain, Normality, and the Struggle for Congruence: Reinterpreting Residential Care for Children and Youth* (James P. Anglin) The Haworth Press, Inc., 2002, pp. 49-59. Single or multiple copies of this article are available for a fee from The Haworth Document Delivery Service [1-800-HAWORTH, 9:00 a.m. - 5:00 p.m. (EST). E-mail address: docdelivery@haworthpress.com].

http://www.haworthpress.com/store/product.asp?sku=J024
10.1300/J024v24n01_04

The emphasis on personal meanings, social interactions and interpretative process characteristic of a symbolic interactionist perspective is also evident in the formulation of grounded theory (Glaser, 1992, p. 16). The basic aim of grounded theory is to generate theory from social data derived inductively from research in social settings (Strauss & Corbin, 1990, p. 23). Critical to the accomplishment of this purpose is a systematic gathering of data through the active participation of the researcher in the phenomenon of interest. The process of immersion in the data is sometimes referred to by sociologists as "in-dwelling" and most aptly so in relation to a study of group homes. Such data gathering techniques as participant observation, semi-structured interviews, informal conversations, and document analysis are typical of a grounded theory inquiry (Chenitz & Swanson, 1986). Thus, this study was undertaken with a spirit of discovery in pursuit of a contemporary, grounded, and theoretical understanding of group home life and work. The journey did not disappoint the researcher, and it is hoped that the resulting theoretical insights and framework will be of interest and use to others involved in the field of residential group care for young people.

Central to the grounded theory method is the search for a main theme, often referred to in the research literature as a "core category" or "core variable" in relation to which most other aspects of the phenomenon of interest can be understood and explained. As Glaser states, "The goal of grounded theory is to generate a theory that accounts for a pattern of behavior which is relevant and problematic for those involved" (1978, p. 93). Similarly, Strauss comments that "the analyst constantly looks for the main theme, for what appears to be the main concern of or problem for the people in the setting . . ." (1987, p. 35). Typically, many compelling themes and categories emerge over the course of a study; some almost immediately and some at various points along the way. As happened in this study, a category's full integrating significance may not become evident until somewhat later in the research process after a great deal of analysis is done. Over a period of many months, a number of themes may vie in the researcher's mind for the ultimate status of "core," and the analytic challenge is to sort through the pretenders to the title and to continue the search until a "true" core is found. A key test for a core category is its ability to integrate the other major categories into a coherent and dense theoretical framework (Glaser, 1978, pp. 120-123). Once the core category is identified, it is articulated and explored in terms of its associated properties and sub-categories, resulting in a theoretical model that in an applied context such as group home life and work can serve as an heuristic device for both enhanced practice and further significant research.

In the grounded theory method, the researcher is searching the data on a continual and comparative basis in order to discover a core category, or core variable, that will serve to connect and place in perspective virtually all of the elements of the phenomenon being studied. To those unfamiliar with the grounded theory approach, this requirement can seem unreasonable and unattainable. How can one category or variable be expected to connect or explain all facets of a complex phenomenon such as the functioning of a group home? Glaser (1992, p. 79) and Strauss (Strauss & Corbin, 1990, p. 121) both acknowledge that there can be several almost equally compelling candidates for selection as the core category. In fact, several theoretical formulations could be constructed, each beginning with a different variable as central, and the other major elements being included as sub-categories of the one selected as core. Also, depending upon the researcher's own sensitivities (Glaser, 1978, p. 1; Strauss & Corbin, 1990, pp. 42-43), it is likely that different themes or categories may be highlighted from the data collected and, indeed, different data will almost surely be collected as a result. Therefore, while there should be close correspondences between the elements of different theoretical formulations concerning the same phenomenon, there is no one "right" or "true" theory about social phenomena. Rather, what is important is that relevant data are gathered and that the categories that emerge within a research study indeed fit the data and help to explicate important problematics for participants engaged within these phenomena.

In this research study of group homes, several variables emerged as vitally important to understanding group home life and group home work. To some degree, these variables related to the various core problems encountered by participants at different levels and occupying different roles within the home. For a period of time, it appeared that no one variable could adequately encompass the other major variables and be deemed "core," and that several variables would need to be given equal weight and emphasis. However, eventually it became apparent that one concept indeed did occupy an overarching position in relation to the others and, through its integrating power, it could make clear the linkages between all of the identified key categories. Thus, the three remaining categories, while central to an understanding of specific problems identified in group home life and work, became sub-categories, and their systematic interrelations and relationship to the core category could then be readily defined. As stated by Glaser (1998, p. 190), "The smaller the amount of concepts that account for the greatest variation in substantive behavior resolving the main concern is the goal."

The basic elements of the theoretical framework resulting from the application of the grounded theory method in this study will now be set out in summary form. In subsequent chapters, an in-depth exploration of the core category—its properties and sub-categories—will be presented in the context of the data on which they are grounded. Figure 1, the Framework Matrix for Understanding Group Home Life and Work, graphically illustrates the theoretical elements of the framework and suggests, with its rectangular cube and sub-cubes encompassed within an oval design, the degree of their key linkages and interrelations.

THE CORE CATEGORY AND THEME

The category that was found to permeate the data across all of the homes and that encompassed the other major categories was *congruence in service of the children's best interests.* As will be demonstrated in subsequent chapters, this core variable provides both a theoretical and practical touchstone for understanding and assessing virtually all other group home elements, their significance, and their patterns of interrelation within group home life and work.

While the notion of *congruence* was included in the set of questions formulated in the initial proposal for this study, the researcher had little idea of its nature, characteristics, and relationship to other elements and did not grasp its ultimate centrality and significance in a theoretical understanding of group home functioning. Such an understanding emerged late in the study.

A group home may demonstrate congruence or incongruence to varying degrees across its elements, processes, and overall operation, and it may do so with a variety of *congruence orientations.* For example, there may be an orientation toward operational efficiency, to the preferences of the staff, or to reducing the budget. In actuality, there are always competing interests and intentions within an organization as complex as a group home, and *full congruence* throughout an organization can best be understood as an ideal state never actually achieved in reality.

In this study, each home was found to be engaged in what could be termed a *struggle for congruence,* and what was discovered to be at the center of most of the struggles was the intention to serve "the children's best interests." Related and virtually synonymous terms such as "child-centered" and "child-oriented" were also used by research participants to express this notion, but *the children's best interests* wording seemed most precise and evocative of the ideal being sought in practice. At the same time, while most of the homes in this study gave at least some evidence of holding this goal as an ideal, some of the homes clearly were not being guided in their work by such a focus. Further, no home was fully consistent in making all decisions on this basis (nor could one expect them to be), given both the competing interests that form the reality of group home operation and the natural variability of staff in their understandings and abilities to achieve congruence in their actions. As will be seen over the course of the analyses and discussions to follow, there are types of deci-

FIGURE 1. Framework Matrix for Understanding Group Home Life and Work

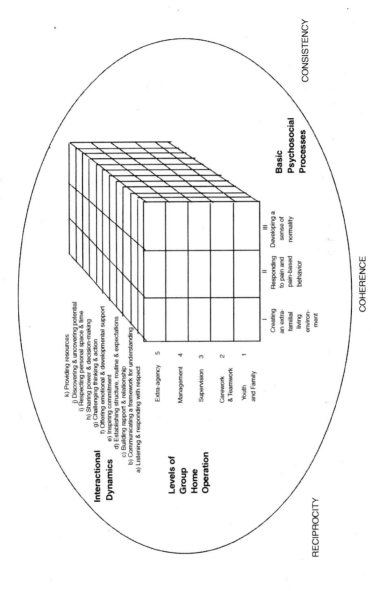

sions and aspects of decision-making in which the predominant concern must be the child's or children's best interests in order for a home to be considered well-functioning, at least in terms of addressing the needs of the residents and their families.

The concept of *children's best interests* has become a widely accepted notion in international instruments such as the United Nations Convention on the Rights of the Child (United Nations, 1989) as well as in the child welfare and child protection literatures in North America and the United Kingdom (Alston, 1994; Goldstein, Freud & Solnit, 1973, 1979). It is interesting to note that even the first book on residential child and youth care published in North America by August Aichhorn (1935) includes the notion of acting "in the child's interest" (p. 194) as a touchstone for child and youth care practice. Therefore, it should not be too surprising that this longstanding and currently dominant concept was echoed in the words of some of the supervisors and managers of homes and agencies within the research sample.

Other major competing interests observed within the homes and present in all homes to varying degrees and in various manifestations include cost containment, worker preferences, and maintaining control. For example, in one home (Parke Street) *maintaining control of the youth* was a dominant theme, whereas in another (Pioneer Place) the focus was on a *manager's efforts to maintain control* of the staff and the mode of operation of the home. In both instances, these efforts to *maintain control* were seen to be competing in multiple ways with serving *the best interests* of the residents, resulting in a strong sense of incongruence within the culture of these two homes.

In summary, and as will be explored in more detail in subsequent chapters, it was evident throughout this study that the core challenge for the group homes studied was to achieve *congruence in service of the children's best interests*. The specific processes and interactions found to be most significant in creating such congruence will now be outlined.

BASIC PSYCHOSOCIAL PROCESSES

In grounded theory, the terms *basic social process* (BSP), and *basic social psychological process* (BSPP) are used to designate those processes that have considerable explanatory power in relation to the phenomenon being studied (Chenitz & Swanson, 1986, p. 134; Glaser, 1978, p. 102). The more common and compact term "psychosocial" will be used here in lieu of "social psychological" to refer to processes that combine in an integral manner both individual and collective elements. The ongoing comparative analysis of the data generated in this study revealed three dominant and pervasive psychosocial processes related to the central problematic of the *struggle for congruence in service of the children's best interests*. While each process is subsidiary to the main theme, each could also be viewed as a core category in its own right in relation to a sub-problem within group home life and work.

The Extrafamilial Living Environment

The most general or pervasive psychosocial process identified is creating an extrafamilial living environment, pertaining to the overall development and ongoing operation of a group home. The notion of an extrafamilial living environment, or "extrafamilial home," captures a fundamental tension inherent in this form of setting and helps to clarify the group home's unique nature in juxtaposition to foster care and institutional care on the continuum of residential services. As its name implies, a group home strives to offer a home-like environment not attainable within an institutional setting while removing the intimacy and intensity of a family environment. Much of the ongoing confusion and disagreement concerning the need for group homes can be attributed to a lack of appreciation of the importance of the "extrafamilial home" dimension. In this study, and as will be explored in some depth in a later chapter, group home managers and staff themselves frequently did not grasp the significance of this defining aspect of group home life.

Responding to Pain and Pain-Based Behavior

Responding to pain and pain-based behavior is the primary challenge at the level of the carework staff. While the residential child and youth care literature frequently mentions the "troubled and troubling" nature of the youth in care (for example, Hobbs, 1982), and acknowledges their traumatic backgrounds, there is a tendency to "gloss over" the deep-seated and often long-standing pain carried by these youth. The term "pain-based behavior" has been coined to remind us that so-called "acting out" behavior and internalizing processes such as "depression" are very frequently the result of a triggering of this internalized pain. Perhaps more than any other dimension of the carework task, the ongoing challenge of dealing with such primary pain without unnecessarily inflicting secondary pain experiences on the residents through punitive or controlling reactions can be seen to be the central problematic for the carework staff.

One of the observed characteristics of staff in a well-functioning home is a sensitivity to the need to respond effectively and sensitively to both the youth residents' behavior and their own personal anxieties. At the same time, few managers, supervisors, and staff demonstrate an understanding of the underlying pain in the residents and within themselves. When it is brought to their attention, there is often a remembrance of the experience of pain, both the residents' and their own, and a realization that they have let this experience slide beneath their ongoing awareness. This intensive psychosocial process, and its frequent repression, makes acting in the best interests of the residents very difficult and represents perhaps the greatest potential barrier to achieving a high level of congruence within the home in service of the children's best interests.

Developing a Sense of Normality

Developing a sense of normality operates at the level of the residents and is the third basic psychosocial process. As will be discussed in a later chapter, this psychosocial process not only captures the central task, or goal, to be accomplished by the residents, it also serves to define a key element of what constitutes the resident children's best interests. There is an apparent paradox at the heart of this process that can be confusing and worrisome to critics of group home care. How can an "abnormal" (or "artificial") living environment such as a staffed group home foster the development of normality? Won't the residents simply become institutionalized in such an extrafamilial context? As will be discussed later in Chapter 7, what a well-functioning group home can offer residents is *a sense of* normality, thus providing a bridging experience in terms of the resident's readiness to engage successfully in more normative environments.

As has already been emphasized, each of these three psychosocial processes is closely interrelated with the others, and in reality they exist as coterminous interwoven threads or interrelated facets of the overall struggle for congruence within a home. To illustrate this point, a significant factor in a resident's experience of developing a sense of normality will be the manner in which staff respond to his pain and pain-based behavior in the course of creating and shaping the extrafamilial living environment. Further, these pervasive psychosocial processes are made up of many moment-by-moment interactions between individuals, and some of the most pervasive and pivotal of these interactional dynamics will be outlined next. These interactional dynamics provide an important means for understanding and assessing the degree of congruence throughout a group home organization and its functioning.

INTERACTIONAL DYNAMICS

On the basis of a comparative analysis of the interpersonal interactions occurring within the homes as noted during the on-site visits and discussed in interviews, eleven dynamics emerged as most pervasive and influential. This category of *interactional dynamics* identifies the most significant modes of relation between persons within and connected to the group home. These interactional dynamics can be understood as the key relational ingredients of group home life and work and as elements of the larger psychosocial processes already identified. Briefly stated, the dynamics include:

1. listening and responding with respect;
2. communicating a framework for understanding;
3. building rapport and relationship;
4. establishing structure, routine and expectations;
5. inspiring commitment;
6. offering emotional and developmental support;
7. challenging thinking and action;
8. sharing power and decision-making;
9. respecting personal space and time;
10. discovering and uncovering potential; and
11. providing resources.

As will be seen in subsequent chapters, each of these interactional dynamics can come together with various others in a single moment or episode, much in the same way as various ingredients combine in the preparation of different culinary preparations. The creation of a resident's best interests environment can be seen to be largely a matter of combining these interactional ingredients in a highly congruent manner while sensitively addressing the three major and intertwined psychosocial processes of creating the extrafamilial living environment, responding to pain and pain-based behavior, and developing a sense of normality.

Finally, one additional category was also found to be important in completing the framework for understanding group home functioning, namely, the levels of group home operation.

LEVELS OF GROUP HOME OPERATION

Organizations such as group homes are not simply assemblages of people, paper, procedures, and premises. As the term "organization" suggests, these elements must be brought together in an organized fashion. As with most such settings, group homes consist of a hierarchy of operating levels, or domains, each with its defined set of roles and responsibilities. In this study, five such levels were clearly evident as reflected in participants' ongoing thinking and action within the homes.

1. Extra-agency level (e.g., contracting, funding, liaison);
2. Management level (e.g., administration, budgeting, resource allocation, personnel management);
3. Supervision level (e.g., overseeing careworkers, team development, programming, resident care);
4. Carework and teamwork level (e.g., working individually and collectively with youth and family members, completing reports, linking with community agencies);
5. Youth resident and family level (e.g., daily living, visiting).

The word "levels" rather than "domains" will be used to reflect more explicitly the hierarchical nature of these operational dimensions. In the next chapter, the notion of a "flow of congruence" from the higher levels to the lower levels will be identified and explored as an important aspect of the core category of congruence in service of the children's best interests and how it comes to be realized (or not) in actual practice.

SUMMARY

The core variable and central theme that permeates the research data in this study is congruence in service of the children's best interests. Three basic psychosocial processes have been identified as being important and systematically linked to the actualization of this variable, namely, creating an extrafamilial living environment, responding to pain and pain-based behavior, and developing a sense of normality. Further, eleven interactional dynamics emerged from the comparative analysis as constituting these processes in the moments, episodes, and relationships of group home life and work, and all of these dynamics were evident within and across each of the five levels of home operation as experienced by the participants: the extra-agency level, management level, supervision level, carework and teamwork level, and youth residents and families level.

As will be demonstrated in subsequent chapters, the degree to which a group home is functioning well or poorly can be examined by viewing these elements and their various juxtapositions through the lens of the central theme: congruence in service of the resident children's best interests. A home may be characterized by high levels of congruence but may be primarily focused on the needs or preferences of the staff or the interests of the organization. Alternatively, staff in a home may have the intention of meeting the best interests of the residents but may encounter or create an insufficient degree of congruence throughout the organization to achieve this goal.

It is proposed that this theoretical framework can assist not only in determining the degree to which a group home is well-functioning or poorly functioning but also in identifying areas of specific strength and weakness. Thus, it offers a theoretical tool grounded in the realities of group home life and work to assist in enhancing practice, drafting sensitive policies, targeting standards, ensuring the relevance of education and training, focusing research, and guiding evaluation. The following chapter will examine the central integrating theme of the framework in the context of the data gathered and the process of analysis undertaken.

Chapter 4

Congruence in Service
of the Children's Best Interests:
The Central Theme
of Group Home Life and Work

This method seems to contradict the present popular belief that the best education means letting the child do as he likes. . . . We consider that these continual limitations of his freedom are in the child's interest. . . .

–August Aichhorn (1935, p. 194)

In all actions concerning children, whether undertaken by public or private social welfare institutions, courts of law, administrative authorities or legislative bodies, the best interests of the child shall be a primary consideration.

–Article 3(1), United Nations Convention
on the Rights of the Child (1989)

A central problematic for group home participants and thus for this research is the question, "What makes a well-functioning group home?" It is important to distinguish this question from another question: "What does a good group home look like?" This latter question could, at least in theory, be addressed by offering a static description, essentially presenting a "slice of life" image. The former question, and the one of greater interest in this study, calls for a dynamic analysis of processes and interactions over time. Thus, the core variable needs to be understood as a vibrant theme, or as a connecting and resonating

[Haworth co-indexing entry note]: "Congruence in Service of the Children's Best Interests: The Central Theme of Group Home Life and Work." Anglin, James P. Co-published simultaneously in *Child & Youth Services* (The Haworth Press, Inc.) Vol. 24, No. 1/2, 2002, pp. 61-78; and: *Pain, Normality, and the Struggle for Congruence: Reinterpreting Residential Care for Children and Youth* (James P. Anglin) The Haworth Press, Inc., 2002, pp. 61-78. Single or multiple copies of this article are available for a fee from The Haworth Document Delivery Service [1-800-HAWORTH, 9:00 a.m. - 5:00 p.m. (EST). E-mail address: docdelivery@haworthpress.com].

http://www.haworthpress.com/store/product.asp?sku=J024
10.1300/J024v24n01_05

thread, running through the ongoing life and work within a group home setting.

CONGRUENCE

The theme that was found to permeate the data across all of the homes and that served to connect and integrate all of the other major categories identified was congruence. As will be demonstrated in subsequent chapters, this core theme provides the theoretical touchstone by which one can understand the significance of virtually all of the other group home elements and processes as well as their patterns of interrelation and interdependence.

When this study was initially conceptualized, the notion of congruence was included as one of the aspects of interest to the researcher in the data gathering process. The inclusion of this concept was based upon both direct and indirect experiences with group home settings over a period of twenty-five years and could be characterized as a form of "hunch" or, at best, as a vague hypothesis. However, while there was growing evidence as the study progressed of the existence of patterns related to behavioral and organizational congruence and incongruence, within and across the various homes, it was not until quite late in the analysis that the central and integrative nature of this category became fully apparent. When all of the major categories were compared in some detail in terms of their properties, interconnections and significance, the theme of congruence emerged as the most pervasive and integrative.

Criteria for Identifying a Core Category

Glaser (1978) has proposed a set of eleven criteria by which a core category can be determined (pp. 95-96). Each of these criteria will be reviewed in relation to the concept of congruence as uncovered in this study.

1. *It must be central.* That is, it must be related to as many other categories and their properties as possible and more so than the other candidates for the core category. This criterion indicates that the category accounts for a large portion of the variation in the pattern of behavior characteristic of the social phenomenon of interest. As will be reflected in this and subsequent chapters, the category of congruence was seen to link readily with all other major variables that also emerged over the course of the extensive process of data gathering and analysis.

2. *It must recur frequently in the data.* The notion of congruence (which will be further defined) was found to permeate the data collected in all of the homes and continually over time.

3. *It takes more time to saturate than the other categories.* Given that congruence permeated virtually all elements and processes within the data, considerably more time was spent in analyzing its properties and relations to other categories.

4. *It relates meaningfully and easily with other categories,* and the connections are readily evident. As noted in point 1 above, this was indeed the case.

5. *It has clear and "grabbing" implications for formal theory.* Formal theory is theory that transcends a merely substantive focus. For example, a variable central to one form of organization such as group homes may be seen as relevant to an understanding of organizations in general. As a result of the analysis undertaken in this study, the researcher has been able to apply the notion of congruence usefully to an analysis of the functioning of other organizations, such as a government division and a university department. Glaser uses the term "grab" or "grabbing" to refer to the fact that a notion captures one's thinking or imagination beyond its immediate use or meaning.

6. *It has "carry-through."* That is, by its relevance and explanatory power, it moves the analyst through the data rather than leading to a dead-end. The process of analyzing the major categories was initially experienced as a somewhat confusing and halting task but proceeded more steadily and smoothly once the category of congruence was identified as core.

7. *It is highly variable due to its dependence on related categories.* As will become evident in subsequent chapters, the nature and degree of congruence within a group home environment varies readily with changes in the related major categories.

8. *While accounting for variation in the problematic behavior, the core category is also a dimension of the problem.* Certainly, the struggle for congruence was observed to be central to the problem of creating a well-functioning group home over the course of the study and throughout the ongoing comparative analysis.

9. *A core category should prevent ungrounded sources from dominating the analysis.* While the category of congruence was embedded in the initial research questions, it was not seriously considered as a candidate for core until its pervasive presence, integrative power, and explanatory relevance became evident to the researcher. No ungrounded category derived from other studies or theories proved to be as powerful and integrative as congruence, and thus could not unduly distract the attention of the researcher.

10. *Because of its "grab" and explanatory power, it can tempt the researcher to see its presence in all relations, whether grounded or not.* While the full significance of the category of congruence took a while to emerge, the tendency to prematurely force the construct on the data has been resisted by

systematically ensuring that all analyses of the category, and its properties and relations, have been well-grounded in the study data.

11. *The core category may be any kind of theoretical code (i.e., concept)* such as a process, a condition, a strategy, a consequence, and so forth. In fact, it would appear that the category of "congruence" could be understood and explored within several such codes, for example, as a *condition* of an organization or as a *consequence* of certain actions within an organization.

Congruence within the context of this study well meets all of the criteria identified as necessary for being considered as the core category, variable, or theme. But what exactly is meant by the term "congruence"? On the basis of an analysis of relevant data, the category of congruence was found to encompass three major properties: consistency, reciprocity, and coherence.

Consistency refers to the degree to which the same set of values, principles, processes, or actions are demonstrated in practice over time and within and across the various dimensions, levels, and domains of group home operation. Throughout this study, as will be explored in each of the chapters on the key psychosocial processes, the notion of achieving consistency was seen to be problematic in relation to each level of group home operation. The levels identified include the experiences of youth and families, the behavior of individual staff members, the functioning of a team (including the work of the supervisor), the actions of management, and the linkages with outside agencies and professionals.

At the level of the individual, for example, the youth residents expect each staff member to treat them in a consistent manner over time as well as according to their individual needs and wants. At the level of staff functioning as a team, there is also an ongoing struggle to ensure sufficient consistency across staff members while at the same time allowing for individual differences in working style, relationship, and approach. The task of ensuring staff consistency was seen by several agency managers to be an important responsibility of the home supervisor, and a pronounced lack of consistency between a manager and a supervisor in one setting was seen to result in negative attitudes and a lowered quality of work of the supervisor and also the staff members. Ultimately, and as will be illustrated later in this chapter, the post-discharge lives and behaviors of the youth were also seen to reflect the consistency or lack of consistency with which the philosophy characteristic of a home (to the degree that there was one) was implemented.

Reciprocity as a property of congruence is understood in this context as the degree of mutuality demonstrated in the interactions between persons involved with and within the home. Thus, when interactions are reciprocal, there is a significant degree of commonality between what is intended and what is received in the communication process, as well as an experience of the two-way relationship in the behaviors exhibited. This reciprocal element of congruence will be more fully explored below in the context of the eleven interactional dynamics that emerged as most significant and pervasive in the struggle for congruence.

Finally, *coherence* refers to the degree to which all of the behaviors and activities of an individual, a group (or team), the home, or system of care have an overall sense of wholeness and integrity. In a team situation, this coherence is sometimes referred to as cohesiveness.

A worker from Oriole emphasized the direct linkage between team cohesion and the impact on the residents.

> If we are a cohesive team, and things go well, and we communicate really well, the kids see that. The mutual respect, no hierarchy, and [hierarchy] is how these kids see much of their lives. . . . At the other place [group home], kids go around staff to the "boss" supervisor. . . .

Thus, the notion of coherence can be understood as a form of summative evaluation of a unit occurring within group home life and work such as an individual person, a staff team, a home, or the entire group home system. Whereas the degree of consistency and reciprocity can be examined in relation to individual actions and interactions, coherence can only be determined by stepping back and reviewing the overall pattern of actions and interactions. It is a term that describes the "forest" rather than the individual "trees."

It is perhaps important to emphasize at this point in the discussion that different group homes could all rate highly on congruence but in very different ways. There are always competing interests and intentions within an organization as complex as a group home, and it is evident that full congruence (whatever its focus may be) is an ideal state that is never completely achieved. Thus, one can more usefully and accurately speak of degrees of congruence (or incongruence).

THE STRUGGLE FOR CONGRUENCE

As mentioned in the previous paragraph, full congruence in a staffed group home, as in any other complex organization, should be viewed as an ideal state or goal, but it is never fully achieved. Therefore, rather than demanding the unattainable, perhaps we should heed the recommendation of Winnicott (1986, pp. 119-120) concerning the aim of achieving "good enough" mothering and "good enough" care, also adapted by Bettelheim (1988, p. xi) in relation to being "good enough" parents, and consider that what is likely to be achieved in most instances in the struggle for congruence is not a perfect, or even a well-functioning home, but rather a "good enough" or "well-enough function-ing" group home.

It became evident as this study progressed that, in order for a group home to operate in even a "well-enough functioning" manner, the eleven interactional dynamics introduced briefly in the previous chapter needed to be present in a largely congruent manner at and across all levels of the organization: ex-tra-agency, managerial, supervisory, carework/team, and (to at least an ever increasing extent) youth and family.

The following charts draw upon an analysis of the observations and inter-views carried out in this study in order to illustrate some of the ways in which each of the core interactional dynamics was seen to form a pattern in the better functioning group homes at the various operational levels. The youth level is included to indicate the kinds of behaviors that were observed to gradually in-crease once the youth residents had begun to respond to what can now be re-ferred to as "good-enough carework" within a well-enough functioning setting. (The impacts of these eleven dynamics on the resident's growth and develop-ment will be examined in more detail in Chapter 7, when the primary goal for residents will be explored.)

1. Listening and Responding with Respect

Contractual level: Ministry contract worker seeks to

a) understand agency contractor's expertise and point of view, and
b) respond respectfully during negotiations and when problems arise.

Managerial level: management seeks supervisor and worker input and responds promptly and effectively to needs and concerns.

Supervisory level: supervisor actively engages staff in an open and attentive manner and takes their points of view into account in planning and decision-making.

Carework level: youth are given attention and their perspectives and experiences are sought out and actively taken into account, with reasons offered for decisions.

Youth level: youth begin to substitute words for acting out or withdrawal and to engage in decision-making and problem-solving interactions with staff and other residents.

— erase first pg!

— Approx (35) pg
have hL'g

Ask me!
o

2. Communicating a Framework for Understanding

Contractual level: clear specification of the type of services to be provided and the population to be served, a comprehensive outline of the standards to be met, and the operational and casework procedures to be followed.

Managerial level: an explicit guiding operational, developmental, and therapeutic philosophy, and clear principles, policies, and procedures made available to staff along with adequate orientation and in-service training.

Supervisory level: clearly communicated professional expectations for all major aspects of staff and home functioning including teamwork guidelines and regular team meetings, individual staff development objectives, and personalized resident goals.

Carework level: working within children's rights, principles, and home rules, routines and expectations shared with the residents, behavioral guidelines for both staff and residents, and discussion with residents of the reasons for actions taken by staff.

Youth level: reinforce home guidelines and expectations amongst each other and with newcomers, and able to articulate—and "own"—their personal developmental goals relating to their being in the home.

3. Building Rapport and Relationships

Contractual level: a respectful and open contractual relationship between governmental representatives and agency leadership to ensure mutual accountability and focus on the provision of appropriate and quality services for youth and their families.

Managerial level: respectful, collaborative, and open management relations with supervisory and carework staff ensuring mutual accountability and a focus on the children's best interests.

Supervisory level: respectful, collegial, and open worker-supervisor relations ensuring mutual accountability and sensitive, appropriate, and effective carework focused on the residents' best interests.

Carework level: respectful, caring, and engaging worker-resident relationships ensuring a good quality of group home life and healing, growth, and development for residents, including in their family relationships.

Youth level: positive and respectful relationships with peers, family members, staff members, and significant others in community services.

4. Establishing Structure, Routine, and Expectations

Contractual level: clear "request for proposal" process and well-defined guidelines, standards of practice, and quality assurance processes followed through with administrative fairness.

Managerial level: program philosophy, operational policies, job responsibilities, performance review procedures, complaints procedures, and so forth, evident to staff members.

Supervisory level: individual worker and team guidelines and expectations, regular staff meetings, appropriate training and personnel policies, and feedback and complaint processes evident to staff members.

Carework level: house routines, rules, and procedures communicated "with expectation in their (staff member's) voice."

Youth level: begin to take charge of some of their own daily life and "case" planning and contribute to group and home decision-making.

5. Inspiring Commitment

Contractual level: communicate a sense of social responsibility and worthiness for the task of providing residential services for children and their families.

Managerial level: stimulate a sense of pride in the integrity of the agency and the worthiness of the group home program.

Supervisory level: foster a sense of team spirit and individual self-worth in and among the careworkers and in their involvement with residents, residents' families, and allied professionals and community resources.

Carework level: foster a positive group atmosphere within the home and a sense of personal self-worth and hope for the future amongst residents and their families.

Youth level: demonstrate cooperation in group home setting and look positively towards the future.

6. Offering Emotional and Developmental Support

Contractual level: recognize the value of and provide tangible resources for agency and staff development initiatives.

Managerial level: recognize the value of and provide resources for group home and staff development activities (including for the supervisor).

Supervisory level: offer psychological, emotional and tangible support for the staff team and individual workers to pursue developmental goals.

Carework level: through ongoing personal interactions, engage residents and family members in supportive relationships characterized by respect and dialogue.

Youth level: interact with others in an empathic manner.

7. Challenging Thinking and Action

Contractual level: dialogue focused on clarification of agency's contract proposal and service orientation before a contract is signed, and period-ically thereafter, with a focus on ensuring the children's best interests.

Managerial level: discussion, reflection, and questioning on a periodic and regular basis concerning the agency philosophy and group home orientation—and their implementation—with a focus on ensuring the children's best interests.

Supervisory level: raise questions related to the intent and effectiveness of staff actions and thereby assist in the development of a practice approach in service of the children's best interests on the part of staff.

Carework level: careworkers raise questions related to the intent and effectiveness of their own and each other's actions, thereby assisting them to become more conscious of their decisions, intentions, and their options for action.

Youth level: speak out on their own behalf and advocate appropriately for others.

8. Sharing Power and Decision-Making

Contractual level: while the final decisions related to the contracts lie with the Ministry, the terms of agreement are negotiated in a transparent and good-faith manner with agencies.

Managerial level: oversees the work of home supervisors while allowing them room to exercise their professional expertise and judgment in supervising staff.

Supervisory level: oversee the work of staff within the homes and encourage them to make decisions within their sphere of understanding and responsibility while ensuring resident safety, well-being, and best interests.

Carework level: oversee the daily lives of the residents, encouraging them to assume responsibility for their own behavior and to make decisions commensurate with their developing capacities.

Youth level: acknowledge the rights and responsibilities of self and others.

9. Respecting Personal Space and Time

Contractual level: government workers collaborate with group home director/manager, showing sensitivity to the processes and pace of agency operation and group home development.

Managerial level: agency managers work collaboratively with home supervisors, showing sensitivity to the processes and pace of staff and program development.

Supervisory level: supervisors work collaboratively with staff within mutually agreed-upon goals and professional development objectives, sensitive to individual differences.

Carework level: careworkers respond sensitively to the inner and outer experiences and realities of youth residents while fostering the development of personal goals at their own appropriate developmental and therapeutic pace.

Youth level: youth begin to accept themselves, their peers, and family members for who they are and where they are developmentally.

10. Discovering and Uncovering Potential

Contractual level: understand and put into place contracts on the basis of a system of care that enables each agency and group home to function at its optimum level.

Managerial level: hire experienced and skilled supervisors and enable them with adequate resources, support, and responsibility to create a well-functioning staff team.

Supervisory level: ensure that staff develop a sense of their strengths and areas for growth, and that they pursue opportunities for personal and professional development.

Carework level: create opportunities for youth to experience their strengths, to heal their brokenness, to learn and grow across all developmental areas, and to develop a sense of achieving their destiny rather than being victims of fate.

Youth level: begin to take new developmental risks, cooperate with others, and to show a sense of mutual responsibility.

11. Providing Resources

Contractual level: allocate funds and other resources (e.g., staff training or consultation) to develop agency services and group homes in the system of care.

Managerial level: provide supervisors and workers with the resources (time, equipment, and money) necessary to accomplish the home objectives.

Supervisory level: spend sufficient individual and team time in mentoring the knowledge, skills, and self-development necessary for quality work and worker satisfaction.

Carework level: to spend sufficient, focused time with individual youth and the resident group and to participate in and support activities designed to support youth to achieve their personal goals.

Youth level: begin to participate in new and developmentally appropriate activities and begin to assist others.

In addition to the identification of various elements in the struggle for congruence, it also became apparent that there existed "a cascading effect" that invariably happened in only one direction: from the higher levels of the organizational hierarchy to the lower ones. In the context of the main theme, this phenomenon was termed *the flow of congruence* and, fortunately, it was observed in this study to occur more often in positive ways than in negative ones.

The Flow of Congruence

An analysis of interview transcripts and observations across the various levels of operation within the life of the homes indicated a strong tendency for the philosophy and practice orientation of the home manager to permeate through the rest of the home and even into the experiences and ways of thinking of youth residents. Extra-home contacts, including the Ministry staff and allied professionals in the community, often picked up many of these messages as well. The following representative excerpts drawn from interviews undertaken in relation to the Yellowdale home offer an illustration of such a flow of congruence. A consistency in the use of cognitively-oriented concepts and principles and an emphasis on behavior change through rethinking and achieving different understanding is evident at all levels of the group home operation. The key words and phrases indicating this cognitive-behavioral orientation are italicized within the quotes for emphasis.

Yellowdale manager/supervisor:

> We help kids to *use their own controls*. We use structure and environment management: arranged chaos! . . . I am not one for consequences based just on behaviors. *I want to know* what is creating this behavior. I want to help the kid to *learn and manage* what is going on. It is harder than grounding or taking away privileges. It is more work to *work things through*. . . . The talking we do here is quite surprising to the kids; they are not used to that. *In my thinking* and work, I do a lot of reading and research. . . . We need to work together *to learn about the kids*, and they need *to learn about us*. *Explanation* is important. . . . I did not want to be another institution, or house. I want to be seen as *a learning opportunity*.

Ministry resource worker speaking about Yellowdale manager/supervisor:

> Well, I think the philosophy is having *a good understanding of the kid*, *knowing about* the kid's problem. . . . They do *a lot of analysis* with the kid's behaviors, motivations, and so on, and *why these kinds of things might be happening*. . . . [The manager] is quite good at identifying those kinds of things . . . and then *strategizing* around them. . . . They do a lot of *problem-solving*; that's their approach with kids. . . . He *thinks things through*.

Male careworker at Yellowdale:

> Well, when something arises, and we say, "No, we're not going to," "We can't go and do that," *we tell them why* we can't do it. There could be physical constraints, time constraints, instead of just saying, "No, you can't do it." But *telling them why* we can't do it, and asking *"Do you understand?"*

Female careworker at Yellowdale:

> We offer *a learning experience* . . . and *I learned* through quite a few . . . scenarios how to step outside my box, and let them [the youth] make the mistake. . . . So, I think [a good staff member here is] someone who *can take theory and put it into practice*, or at least be *open to learning* how to put it into practice.

Second female careworker at Yellowdale:

> You work with it every day . . . sort of *understanding where they're coming from, understanding what's occurred.*

Third female careworker at Yellowdale:

> Yeah, lots of *talking and breaking things down.* [A resident] has, I think, *learned about problem solving.*

Ministry child and family worker speaking about Yellowdale and the Yellowdale manager/supervisor:

> It's a *well thought-out* program and right from the beginning. [The manager] is pretty *knowledgeable.* . . . He had *a fairly good idea* about what didn't work. The emphasis on *teaching kids* responsibility, teaching them coping skills and techniques and mechanisms they need to go back out into society and contend with whatever their own issues are, is really good. . . . The ability to provide that *teaching component* to the parent is essential as well.

Youth resident at Yellowdale:

> Yeah, like say *something's coming on*, like my problem. I go *"I don't want that, like STOP."* Like, it's like slamming a door and stuff. . . . I'd probably remove myself from the situation. Yeah. Either that, or, um, if I can't, I'd just *tell it to go away* and stuff. . . . I like the consequences [here] better than any other place.

Second youth resident at Yellowdale:

> You *realize what you did*, and how much you've done wrong, and *why.* . . .
> *I've learned here* that there [are] better things that you need to do in situ-
> ations . . . *it helped me learn things and understand them* better.

Former resident at Yellowdale:

> I had to write an essay on *why* I ran away, why I wouldn't do it again, and
> every time I did something I shouldn't have done, I had to write an apol-
> ogy letter for it. I had to state what I did, what I'd do next time . . . *it*
> *taught us* basically that in society you can't just get away with a quick
> "sorry," then go out and do it again. *You got to really think* about it.

As illustrated in these brief excerpts, people at all levels of involvement
with the Yellowdale home had learned and could articulate from their own perspective the home manager's philosophy of change. It is particularly interesting that even current and former residents could be very explicit about ways in
which they actually internalized aspects of the approach and philosophy of the
home. While this home could be characterized as having a primarily cognitive-behavioral orientation, other homes studied included those with more af-
fective and relationship-based approaches (Dogwood, Thunderbird, Big House),
more traditional behavior modification methods (Oak Lane, Hillside), environmental structuring (Oriole), narrative therapy (Pioneer Place) and an experiential education/reality therapy orientation (Mountainview). Parke Place,
during the period of observation at least, could best be described as manifest-
ing a custodial approach.

In each instance, the orientation articulated by the manager (or manager/su-
pervisor) could be discerned at each level of the group home operation and
could generally be traced all the way down the organizational hierarchy to the
understandings and behaviors of the youth residents. Whether the flow of congruence was characterized by a developmental, therapeutic, or bureaucratic
orientation or, in one instance, simply by a sense of confusion, negativity, and
inconsistency, the words and actions of the youth residents and former residents frequently demonstrated how they were affected and influenced accordingly. Several recollections by former residents will further illustrate this
phenomenon.

> Standing on top of the mountain, I felt like I was on top of the world; it
> was just great, I loved it. . . . I wouldn't change anything in the program. I
> always saw the good side of it. . . . If they were to put me in the program
> long before my first time getting into trouble, it probably wouldn't have

happened. Now I know I can succeed at things. (Former resident of Mountainview, with an experiential education orientation)

I realized that there were people who saw potential in me, could give me support and back-up that I needed to do it, and guidelines to keep me on the straight and narrow. And I realized that they were actually there to help me as opposed to fight me. . . . [The consequences] were written, so we could think it through. . . . (Former resident of Yellowdale, with a cognitive-behavioral orientation)

I knew that I had a lot of support when I had my overdose, 'cuz . . . I couldn't remember it personally, but everybody told me that [a staff member] showed up before the ambulance got there, and he lives downtown, and so he got there before the ambulance got there, and he drove with me to the hospital in the ambulance. . . . There were staff there twenty-four hours a day for ten days. . . . It was the first place they didn't kick me out of, or that I couldn't get out of. When I was in foster care, as soon as I arrived, I would try to break it down. I'd been moving every three months for seven years. . . . If I hadn't been at Dogwood, I'd still be living in different places for three months at a time. Everybody listened, and I just let go. (Former resident of Dogwood, with a relationship-based orientation)

As mentioned earlier, each home in this study was found to be engaged in "a struggle for congruence." To varying degrees, each group home experienced some pressure to maximize sometimes incompatible aspects of its functioning. For example, and most notably, these competing foci included:

- operational efficiency (e.g., reduce night staff to one from two workers despite added risks to staff and residents);
- preferences of the staff (e.g., wanting shorter shifts to improve their social lives while observing that longer shifts were likely better for the residents);
- cost containment (e.g., cutting recreational and camping trips, knowing that these offered some of the best opportunities for effective carework);
- maintaining control (e.g., utilizing physical restraints instead of taking the time to talk things through or risk damage to the house);
- protecting the community (e.g., situating residents out of town when such a location reduced the developmental and therapeutic opportunities for residents); and
- meeting the needs of the funding Ministry (e.g., giving in to pressure to take inappropriate referrals knowing that they would have a negative impact on the development and treatment of all residents, including the one being referred).

However, congruence is not a category that can stand on its own, and whatever the philosophy of care or change, there must be an overriding aim that guides work within the home. In most of the homes (i.e., the well-enough functioning ones), the primary focus of the struggle for congruence was on maintaining and enhancing the commitment to maximize the children's best interests. However, at the same time, it was certainly the case that some staff (e.g., the manager and several staff at Pioneer Place, a new careworker at Thunderbird, the supervisor at Parke Street) could be seen as giving lip service to the concept without being able to demonstrate a consistent commitment to it in practice.

CHILDREN'S BEST INTERESTS

The concept of children's best interests has become a widely accepted notion in international policy instruments such as the United Nations Convention on the Rights of the Child (1989) as well as in the child welfare and child protection literature (Goldstein, Freud & Solnit, 1973, 1979). The quote from August Aichhorn that appears at the beginning of this chapter is a brief excerpt from what was probably the very first text on residential child and youth care published in North America (Redl & Wineman, 1952, p. 41). It is interesting that Aichhorn's formulation, originally written in German in 1925, contains the notion of "the child's interest" as a primary goal or touchstone of residential work. Therefore, with such deep roots in North American residential literature and such prominent recent attention internationally, perhaps it should not be surprising to find this concept echoed in the words of some of the supervisors, managers and careworkers of homes and agencies within this research sample.

But what does it mean to act in the children's best interests and to put this rhetoric into practice? As the influential text *Before the Best Interests of the Child* states, "Neither law, nor medicine, nor science has magical powers and . . . there is no societal consensus about what is 'best' or even 'good' for all children" (Goldstein, Freud & Solnit, 1979, p. 133). On the basis of the data gathered in this study, it would also be true to say that there is no clear consensus within residential child and youth care practice either. It was evident that each home studied had, to varying degrees of sophistication, their own explicit beliefs (as well as many implicit ones) that together comprised their "theory in use" (Schon, 1983, pp. 305-306) about children's best interests. The reason for this state of affairs can perhaps be explained by the indeterminacy inherent in child and youth care work. As Alston (1994) observes:

According to rational choice theory, in any decision problem a determinate answer will in general require that the following knowledge conditions are satisfied:

1. All the options must be known;
2. All the possible outcomes of each option must be known;
3. The probabilities of each possible outcome occurring must be known; and
4. The value to be attached to each outcome must be known. (p. 29)

It is obvious that it would be a rare situation indeed for all–or even some–of these conditions to be fully satisfied in the context of group homes for young people. Thus, Alston (1994) continues, the meaning of best interests "can depend in large part on localized understanding or conventions" (p. 39). In this study, it was apparent that the standards of care developed at a provincial level (Ministry for Children and Families, 1998) had not yet permeated either the consciousness or practice of the large majority of practitioners. The major exception was the manager of Metro Agency who had participated on the working committee that had overseen the drafting of the standards. However, even in this instance, it did not appear that the staff in her agency had been very thoroughly introduced to the standards document and provisions.

At the same time, it was evident from the in-home observations, informal conversations, and semi-structured interviews that many of the staff who were managing, supervising, and doing carework within the group homes were striving with sincerity and passion to truly serve the best interests of the children on the basis of their own common sense judgements and personal experience. Yet they frequently found themselves struggling with the demands of competing interests and priorities. For example, in one home maintaining control of the youth was a dominant theme emanating from the supervisor, whereas in another the focus was on a manager's efforts to maintain control of the staff and the mode of operation of the home. In both instances, the efforts to maintain control were observed to be competing in multiple ways with serving the best interests of the residents, resulting in a strong sense of incongruence as noted both by a number of staff members within the two homes and confirmed in field visits by the researcher.

SUMMARY

The core challenge for the group homes studied was to achieve congruence in service of the resident children's best interests. An ongoing struggle for congruence was noted within each home as various personal, organizational, and Ministry needs competed with the resident children's best interests. The attainment of full congruence appears not to be achievable in a complex organization such as a group home, and holding to a standard of "well-enough functioning" with a sincere and concerted commitment to meeting the resident children's best interests is perhaps a realistic minimum level of attainment to be expected in the functioning of homes. The hierarchical structure and functioning of the homes was observed to result in a largely one-way flow of congruence from the home manager or manager/supervisor down through the levels of home operation, resulting in observable direct impacts on the developmental and therapeutic outcomes for the residents.

Several of the major psychosocial processes found to be most critical in the struggle for congruence in service of children's best interests will now be explored in the following chapters. Chapter 5 will address the overall task of the homes, Chapter 6 will examine the major challenge for staff members, and Chapter 7 will consider the primary goal for the residents.

Chapter 5
Creating an Extrafamilial Living Environment: The Overall Task of a Group Home

As human actors, the staff members and children who inhabit a residential center do not just *react* to their physical and social environment. In many ways they can be said to *enact* or create it.

–Leon Fulcher (1991, p. 219)

All three of the major psychosocial processes identified at the heart of group home life and work–creating an extrafamilial living environment, responding to pain and pain-based behavior, and developing a sense of normality–are in reality facets of the functioning of a group home, which is one integrated and ongoing process. Therefore, as noted in the quotation from MacMurray (1957) at the beginning of Chapter 3, it is important to remember that only through an analytical process can these processes be separated out from each other at all.

"Creating" refers to the means by which the group home environment is actualized in practice. Each group home, including the group home culture, can be understood as a unique invention shaped by the ideas, intentions, interactions and "hands on" work of many people. The residential child and youth care literature offers a variety of metaphors for this creative process. Quite common are the notions of "constructing" (Barnes, 1991, p. 149) and "structuring" (Clough, 1982, p. 3) the environment, which would be appropriate for a home, but perhaps overly connote the physical and impersonal dimensions to the possible neglect of the psychosocial aspects.

The notion of "crafting" and the perspective that residential child and youth care work can be understood as a "craft" perhaps more appropriately than as an art or a science (at least at this stage of its professional development) has been articulated in the North American literature (Eisikovits & Beker, 1983; Beker &

[Haworth co-indexing entry note]: "Creating an Extrafamilial Living Environment: The Overall Task of a Group Home." Anglin, James P. Co-published simultaneously in *Child & Youth Services* (The Haworth Press, Inc.) Vol. 24, No. 1/2, 2002, pp. 79-105; and: *Pain, Normality, and the Struggle for Congruence: Reinterpreting Residential Care for Children and Youth* (James P. Anglin) The Haworth Press, Inc., 2002, pp. 79-105. Single or multiple copies of this article are available for a fee from The Haworth Document Delivery Service [1-800-HAWORTH, 9:00 a.m. - 5:00 p.m. (EST). E-mail address: docdelivery@haworthpress.com].

http://www.haworthpress.com/store/product.asp?sku=J024
10.1300/J024v24n01_06

Eisikovits, 1991). The notion of a "craft" in relation to professional work has also been discussed for some time in other occupational fields such as social work (Kimball & Partridge, 1979), teaching (Marland, 1975), business (Mintzberg, 1989) and public administration (Berkley, 1980).

Whatever specific creative metaphor may be selected, the central point being made here is that a group home is not simply "found" within a social community; it has to be created, constructed, or crafted. But its creation is not simply a process of construction that is complete once the program statement is drafted, funding is secured, staff members are hired, and the doors are open. Quite the contrary: The creation of a group home entails the ongoing and sensitive shaping of elements that continually evolve and change over time, perhaps in a manner more akin to making pottery than to building a house. David Liederman, a former Executive Director of the Child Welfare League of America, was fond of saying that child welfare work is not rocket science; it's far more complex than that. It requires uncommon sensitivity to human relations.

One of the paradoxical aspects of group home life and work that emerged in this study is that it entails the creation of an *artificial* living environment in order to facilitate the development of a *sense of normality* for the residents. The term "artificial" is used here to denote the fact that group home settings do not preexist naturally in the community as do biological (or "natural") families. One of the defining features of a group home is that its central purpose is to provide an environment specifically crafted to address the needs of referred residents. In foster families, the needs of the adults and other family members are central to the purpose and functioning of these environments, and a child placed in a family home is expected to adapt to a significant degree to the patterns within the family. Indeed, that process of socialization into family life is one of the purposes of using such placements for children who cannot live with their own families. On the other hand, a group home and its staff are in place to offer an environment that will to a significant degree be able to cope with and adjust to the developmental and therapeutic needs of the residents. In this sense, a group home is an *artificial* rather than a *natural* context even though all of the interactions and activities will be real human experiences for all concerned.

While all of the participants in a group home have some role to play in the shaping or crafting process (as in all related psychosocial processes), it was evident in this study that the accomplishment of this task represents the major preoccupation of home managers and supervisors, albeit from somewhat different perspectives. In order to explore the process of creating an extrafamilial ("artificial") living environment in the context of the main theme of congruence in service of the children's best interests, the various physical, structural and process elements of the group home environment will be examined, followed by an exploration of the meaning and significance of its extrafamilial nature.

PHYSICAL AND STRUCTURAL ELEMENTS

Group home settings are different from family homes on a number of significant physical and structural dimensions that will be articulated below. Each of these aspects is crafted and shaped by all of the various participants in the life of the group home, even though the primary responsibility for the overall environment generally lies with the group home manager.

The Physical Setting

Among the most significant elements is the physical setting of the home itself. Eight of the programs studied were located in houses originally built as single family dwellings. From the exterior none of these homes could have been identified as a group care settings. There were no signs indicating that these were any different from any of the other homes on the street. All of these eight homes were surrounded by single-family homes in residential neighborhoods.

The other two settings in the study sample were the Pioneer Place facility and the Mountainview camp. The Pioneer Place residence was built in large part by adult correctional inmates as a work-skills development initiative. It was designed to serve as a group residential facility and was situated in an isolated location within a provincial forest and logging area, about half an hour from a regional hub city. The Mountainview camp, comprising a cluster of mainly log buildings (dormitory, school, kitchen/dining hall, recreation building, woodworking building, sauna, woodshed, and outhouses), was situated on Crown land (land owned by the provincial government) about an hour from a medium-sized urban center.

The three Metro Agency homes (Oriole, Thunderbird, and Dogwood) were all located in different residential neighborhoods in a large city, while the three Valley Agency homes (Parke Street, Big House, and Hillside) were situated in different residential neighborhoods of a medium-sized urban center. Yellowdale was situated in a rural residential community about 40 minutes from the closest city, and Oak Lane was located in a residential neighborhood in a large urban center different from the one that is home to the Metro Agency.

While the exteriors of the residential homes blended in with their surroundings, the interiors conveyed their group care function in a number of ways.

First, all of the ten facilities had at least one staff office, with four of the group homes having two offices allowing for two staff to sleep over at the same time. In addition, all of the settings were equipped with sprinkler systems in case of fire, and several had alarm systems on the doors and windows that could be activated as desired. These alarms were installed primarily to detect residents leaving the premises without permission at night. Unlike some group homes none of the homes in the study had locks on the refrigerators, although there were typically locked food and clothing storage cupboards in the basements or storage areas. One home, Parke Street, had locked bathroom doors, and residents needed a staff member to unlock the door to make use of the facilities. It was not clear if this was a temporary or permanent condition in the home.

All but one of the group home settings in this study had a reasonably pleasant, homey feel to them, with typical home furnishings and a living room, dining area, and kitchen equipped much as a family home would be. The major detractions from the pleasant atmosphere were generally the residents' own rooms that were often quite barren and unkempt. While the unkempt aspect might offer a sense of normality, the sometimes barren walls and a noticeable absence of books, hobbies, games, sports equipment, and the like lacked the sense of variety and richness characteristic of a more engaged lifestyle. Overall, the furnishings and appearance of the homes in this study sample contrasted favorably with a number of other group homes known to the researcher that were less attractively furnished and that were rather poorly maintained, with pieces of battered and broken furniture, dirty walls, and an atmosphere of general neglect.

The Parke Street group home, while a single family dwelling by design, stood out from the others with its office located off the television room with a large observation window installed between them. This configuration gave the home a particularly institutional feel. In all of the other settings, the offices were relatively unobtrusive, much in the way a family den or parent's workspace might be in a family home.

The Mountainview facility, being a camp-style facility, had a dormitory with sixteen beds (including two for staff) in eight double-bunk configurations in one spacious room and a large communal washroom, as well as separate kitchen and dining facilities and outbuildings for sauna, woodworking, weight training, and school. All of these buildings were attractive and well-maintained. The Pioneer Place facility was less home-like than the other group homes, given that it was built to be a group residence. It showed some wear and tear as one would expect being inhabited by eight adolescent boys and located in a rural area where residents trekked in and out with large and often muddy boots.

Another common feature differentiating these homes from family homes was the presence of posted rules, charts, menu lists, point summaries, activity schedules, and other such accoutrements of a planned, group living environment. Sometimes these were confined to the staff offices, but often there were large cork boards with various overlapping notices stapled or pinned at jaunty angles, apparently competing for the limited attention of the passersby. Several of the homes had large chalk boards in communal areas, such as entrance hallways and kitchens. These were used for various purposes, such as listing recreational activities for the week and leaving messages for individual residents or staff. The researcher never became comfortable with instances when personal information, even quite routine aspects such as doctor's appointments or home visits, were displayed on these boards for all visitors to the home to see. The posting of point totals indicating the level of behavior and associated attitudes of residents over the day or week particularly conveyed a sense of artificiality and unnaturalness in the living situation.

The Residents

Given that all but one of these residences were part of the child protection service system (Mountainview being a correctional program), the majority of youth residents had been removed from their families as a result of the neglect or abuse of their parents. In many instances, one of the reasons given for placement was that the young person had been assessed as having serious behavioral problems. The most common behavioral problems noted included aggressive or violent behavior, criminal activities (usually breaking and entering, or theft), substance abuse, sexual acting-out or intrusiveness, depression, attention and/or hyperactivity disorder (ADHD), and chronic running away. Frequently, both inadequate family care or supervision and severe behavioral problems were cited, and characteristically youth residents had been assessed as having multiple problems. Mountainview was the exception, with all residents being referred for conflicts with the law. However, the assessments of these "young offenders" (the term used under Canadian legislation) also included behavioral profiles similar to the residents in the other nine homes.

Behaviors range from frequent foul language, taunting, and insulting exchanges to occasional pokes and "roughhousing." However, over the course of the study, staff encountered two "psychotic breaks," a riot involving broken windows and aggression towards staff, and unauthorized absences, as well as numerous instances of drug and alcohol abuse. While these more troublesome incidents consumed considerable staff energy during and after the periods when they occurred, they were relatively infrequent in most of the homes in the study. In most of these homes, the daily living environment consisted mainly of ongoing "hassles" and the continual need to remind the youth of the elements of civil behavior. This pattern would appear to be indicative of relatively well-functioning homes.

Of the youth living in the settings studied during the course of this research, approximately one-third had been living in their own or a relative's home, one-third in foster homes, and one-third in institutions prior to coming into the group setting. The prior institutional placements included mental health assessment and treatment facilities, and correctional detention centers.

As indicated in Chapter 2, eight of the residential programs examined were staffed group homes with between four and eight beds. The only eight-bed home was specifically for male sex offenders. One of the two remaining programs, Hillside, was a home utilizing a parent live-in model combined with approximately 28 hours weekly of child and youth care staff support for three very challenging boys, one of whom had severe attachment problems and who had been discovered cocaine-addicted and abandoned in a "dumpster" (large rubbish bin) as a baby. The tenth program, Mountainview, was a correctional residential attendance program for 14 boys who had previously been serving sentences for convictions as young offenders.

Clearly, the mix of young people placed in these homes and the persistent demands of their behaviors would represent a quite selective sample of the overall youth population within British Columbia as a whole. Thus, the fact of living extrafamilially in a group care environment would appear to correlate with a resident group exhibiting quite challenging behaviors on an ongoing basis, with periodic incidents of crisis proportion (e.g., psychotic episodes, suicidal behaviors, physical violence, etc.).

The Staff

The carework staff had diverse educational and work experience. Just over one-half of the 35 staff interviewed had university degrees, typically in psychology, education, social work, and criminology but also including some with English, foreign languages, theatre, or other arts or science degrees. Three had a degree and several more had diplomas specifically in child and youth work. One explanation given by a home manager for the small number with a child and youth work credential was the disparity in wages and working conditions between residential care and other youth work positions in schools, community agencies, government mental health facilities, hospitals and family counseling agencies. In the non-urban areas, employers reported relatively few applicants with university-level child and youth care education, despite their desire to have more highly trained workers on staff.

Staff without academic degrees ranged from having some college or university courses or years completed to courses completed at a training institute, and a few with only a high school background. About one-quarter of the staff were either currently pursuing courses at an accredited post-secondary institution or at a training institute that offered certificates and diplomas outside of the accredited university and college system.

Most of the carework staff demonstrated genuine enthusiasm for the work and a passionate commitment to the well-being of the youth residents. The exceptions encountered by the researcher were few, totaling about half a dozen. Significantly, all but one of the staff members interviewed who presented half-heartedly or cynically were in the two homes that were assessed to be poorly functioning. The remaining staff member in this category resigned during an investigation of an incident of physical aggression involving himself and a young resident that occurred over the course of this study. In light of these findings, it would appear that one of the key indicators to look for when considering the quality of a group care program is evidence of genuine and overt enthusiasm for the work. Comments frequently heard from staff in the well-functioning homes were of the following nature: "I *love* working with these kids!"; "I *really* like working with teens, the more off-the-wall the better!"; "I knew that I *always* wanted to work with children in some way."

While a few staff members appeared to be "naturals" in their ability to relate well to the youth and to be able to inspire cooperation and respect without much previous training, the large majority indicated that their learning was a multi-year process and a struggle with gradually developing skill, awareness, and confidence. A worker at Oriole who had been working in residential care for several years and who had just entered a university-based child and youth care academic program described herself as "an adolescent worker . . . I'm still in my adolescence in my own professional development process." While most supervisors would be pleased to hire staff trained in child and youth care or a related discipline, most were resigned to having to hire many workers from outside the helping professions, often with little formal education at all. A supervisor/manager from Oak Lane spoke for several others when she indicated that "a diversity of backgrounds is good: recreation, arts and crafts, outdoors, etc. The degree is important, and it is best if it is more practical." The Oriole supervisor stated simply:

> You need two things to be a great child care worker. You need a very big heart and you need common sense. The rest can be taught. If you haven't got one of those two things, then you are going to be in trouble. And the kids are the ones that do the teaching, right?

Given the complexity and intensity of the needs of the youth in these residential care settings, it is perhaps necessary to question whether such learning on the job through trial and error experiences, while depending largely on the youth to "do the teaching," is either a responsible or suitable way to train residential care staff.

The supervisory staff, managers, and manager/supervisors had a similar educational profile as the carework staff, but they tended to have more years of residential work experience. The average length of time in residential care for the front-line carework staff in this study was just under four years, ranging from a few weeks to over 20 years. For the supervisory staff, the average working life was 11.75 years with an average of 6.25 years in a supervisory capacity. The managers averaged over 10 years in residential care and 7.5 years as managers. Just over one-half of all staff were under 30 years old, and about three-quarters were under 40 years old. Nine percent were 50 years or over. The supervisor and manager group averaged 39 years of age.

In addition to the physical setting, and the characteristics of residents and staff in the group homes, there are a number of processes that also serve to differentiate such homes from family homes in the community.

PROCESS ELEMENTS

First and foremost, the homes in this study differed from more normative homes in the community in that they were brought into being through a process of government contracting. Therefore, the contracting process is an appropriate place to begin an examination of the processes involved in the ongoing creation of an extrafamilial living environment characteristic of group home settings.

Contracting for Group Homes

Typically, the first step in the process of creating a group home is for the Ministry to advertise a Request for Proposals (RFP). In such an RFP, a general description of the age group requiring group care would be specified along with the number of young people to be accommodated and an overview of the type of service being requested (for example, "receiving and assessment," "intensive residential treatment," "long-term care," and the like). Practitioners in the community, referred to as potential "contractors" given the contractual nature of the relationship with the Ministry, would then submit proposals outlining the manner in which they intend to address the specifications in the proposal along with a projected budget. It is usually expected that such elements as program philosophy or orientation, management structure, staffing model and qualifications, shift arrangements, type of setting, and other such aspects of the envisioned operation would be provided.

Each Ministry regional office has workers occupying several related roles who, in some combination, would normally be involved in reviewing the proposals. These roles include a contract manager who is charged with the responsibility of negotiating and drafting the final contract, a resource manager who serves as the ongoing liasion between the Ministry and its resources, and the child and family service workers who provide the case management services to the children placed in such facilities. Practice varies across the regions of the province as to who is involved in the process and to what degree. After all of the proposals have been reviewed, a short list is created and interviews are held with the prospective contractors to discuss the plans in more detail. The contractors may range from an individual who has never before run such a home in the past to a large existing agency already operating a range of residential homes and other social services as well. After a period of discussion and negotiation, a contract is agreed to, and the new home is ready to be initiated.

The contracts for all of the homes in this study were for one year at a time and were subject to annual review and negotiation. In practice, unless there was some major operational problem or a major service policy shift within the Ministry, the contracts were usually renewed with little fanfare. In several instances in this study, a residential child and youth care position was redefined as a family support position, and the number of beds was reduced by one in order to develop a more preventive service orientation. In times of financial cutbacks, budgets could be cut by a certain percentage with agencies being expected to absorb the cost without reducing the level of service. For example, at the start of this study, there was a 2% reduction in group home and social service budgets across the board throughout the province.

It is important to note that even at this early stage in the development of a group home, seeds are being sown that could shape much of what would occur later in terms of the experiences of the residents and the ability of the home to respond to their needs. One of the major influencing factors mentioned by the group home contractors/managers (often the same person) involved in this study was the nature of the relationships developed with the key Ministry staff, usually the contract manager and the resource manager. It was evident that some Ministry contract and resource managers, usually long-time and experienced Ministry workers, took a keen professional and personal interest in both the nature of the proposals and the well-being of the contractors, while others treated the process more like a simple business transaction and a search for the lowest bidder.

The words of the contract manager responsible for Mountainview indicate his concern and his disdain for the "just business" approach evident with some of his counterparts in the Ministry system.

> I think you have to develop a working relationship . . . you know, this idea of an "arms length"–great, okay, but you still have to be able to talk to the [contractors] and give them suggestions, and listen to them when they have something they want to tell you . . . such as what's not working. For example, with another program that provides three foster homes for very difficult kids, [the contractor] is on the phone to me once a week. I don't mind. He's telling me when something is working or not working. If I took the narrow view that we don't provide that under the contract, I'd lose it! I despise the way government treats a lot of programs.

This same contract manager provided several examples of other residential settings operating within his region that he considered unsatisfactory, but there was reluctance at the management level to terminate even poorly functioning programs because "it's easier than finding new ones" to retain them. "We have an outfit up here–it's a disaster! An eight-bed residence, and nobody wants to put a kid in that residence because it's absolute mayhem."

It became evident over the course of this research that not only are some programs not functioning well but most of these are known to the contract managers as poor programs. Yet they are often allowed to continue operating.

> I have been supervising contracts for 20 years now, and for me there is a very clean cut between those that are in the business for the purposes of capital gain [where] the bottom line is the dollar, and those that are in there to help kids. It shows clearly in the product they produce. You see in the ones that are in it for the money, they will cut corners, and not deal with difficult kids, and take other steps to make sure that things will work out for the best financial situation that they can expect. . . . There are a lot of situations where they warehouse kids; there's no real involvement with the kids. They have the kids there, and they don't do much with them. They have "programs" that they fulfill, but they don't interact with the kids.

The same manager also provided a specific example that he used to contrast with Mountainview, which he considered to be a well-functioning residential program.

> An example is behavior modification. If the kid didn't do something, then he gets consequenced . . . very mechanical. The personal involvement is very minimal. Compared to [Mountainview] where you

actually see the staff *with* the kids, *doing* the same things the kids do, and if the kid is sweating and cutting wood, the staff are cutting wood and sweating too. I think there is a difference there, and the kids sense that very quickly, I think. Having been a foster parent myself, hearing the stories of kids going through the various kinds of homes, it's that in one place they feel like a commodity, and in another place they feel like–"hey, these people are out to help us, to do something for us," and that impacts the whole program, regardless of what the fancy framework is.

In this description, the manager demonstrates his familiarity with the Mountainview program as well as some key dynamics observed by the researcher across the sample of homes in this study. The notion that "kids sense things" immediately, the importance of "doing with" residents rather than "doing to" them, as well as an understanding of the various orientations to implementing programs proved to be significant in analyzing the functioning of group homes. These aspects will be further explored in subsequent chapters.

The Ministry manager summed up his experience with the situation at the initiation of a group home succinctly: "The whole program is really designed on the attitude you've got going into creating it." As has been discussed in the previous chapter on congruence, throughout this study the researcher was impressed by the correlation between the attitudes and understandings of the contractors/managers and the way in which the homes functioned overall. The "flow of congruence" proved to be a powerful dynamic that demonstrated the impact "attitudes" had not only on the programs but on the outcomes observed with the residents as well.

The manager of the Metro Agency was quite blunt about the contracting process involved in the initiation of her three group homes: "I think that in all honesty, the Ministry liked the price, and they liked the structure." However, while the cost may have been a factor in the selection of the Metro Agency proposal, and even though the agency was a private, for-profit proprietorship, the quality of the three homes did not reflect the internal cutting of corners decried by Mountainview's Ministry manager. The Metro Agency manager explained her philosophical attitude as follows:

There was over time some of the old child care tension over how behavioral you are and how nurturing you are. People tend to put them on either end of a spectrum, which they are not. So, individual [Ministry] workers would take us on about our AWOL [absent without leave] consequences, or whatever, depending on where they were coming from, and I am a firm believer in positive reinforcement. So there is an incentive system that is the foundation of all of [our] programs, and a very basic system just to sort of, for one, create a structure for staff, so they can form their day and figure out how to work–but also to build on successes. This is what it is all about; "we hope you will form relationships." It was never to be about the incentive system [itself], or compliance.

Thus, a philosophy that focused on the development of staff as well as on the successes of the residents shaped the creation of the Oriole, Dogwood, and Thunderbird homes from the start, and, indeed, this approach was much in evidence throughout the field visits to these homes. The approach to management within the homes can be seen to influence all operations within a home on an ongoing basis, and this aspect will be examined next.

Managing

It was evident over the course of this study that the development of a group home program is not a linear and stable progression from conception to steady-state operation. In fact, if a group home appears to function in a steady-state, it is either stagnant or the observer is not detecting the fact that a well-functioning group home operates on the basis of a dynamic equilibrium. By "dynamic equilibrium" is meant that while change and movement are continuous, there is an underlying structure and harmony that keeps the staff and residents focused on their primary purposes and directions. As with a roller coaster, the reality of a series of ups and downs is not only predictable, it is a necessary part of what the home is all about given the evolution in the needs and experiences of the residents. Of course, it is also possible for a home not to grow and develop but to deteriorate. The manager of Yellowdale, a home that exemplified the dynamic equilibrium characteristic of a well-functioning residence, had also initiated prior to this study a second residence for older teens. However, the complexity of trying to operate a second home as an independent contractor was too much for him to manage successfully, and that program was closed at his request.

Parke Street, operated by the Valley Agency, offered an example of a program that had apparently functioned quite well until it experienced an unplanned "mandate drift" as a result of a shift in the referral practices of the local Ministry office. It was evident that the staff resented the change in emphasis (from short-term assessment to longer-term care), had not been involved in discussions of the change, and had not explored the implications of these shifts in policy and practice for their work and their program approach. The Valley Agency manager had also become quite distant from the home, and the Parke Street supervisor was frustrated and feeling demoralized. As a result, there was not an effective carework team and the youth residents were largely on their own and, on occasion, totally out of control. Over the course of the field work for this study, there occurred what one staff member called "a riot" in which the residents confined the staff to their office, broke a window, and trashed the kitchen and some other parts of the house. As will be explored in a later chapter, other factors such as the supervisor's attitude towards the issue of control also appeared to contribute to the negative culture evident within Parke Street.

In the rest of the residences, a developmental process had been experienced by the managers, supervisors, and long-time staff. Some staff quite enjoyed recalling "war stories" of their earlier experiences in the homes. One careworker at Oriole summed up his experience in graphic terms.

> I like to refer to the old days as "hand to hand combat" or "trench warfare" . . . something like that. . . . It was a war zone. . . . It was a flophouse, plain and simple. Not to be negative, that's what it was. I was new, so I assumed it was normal. I kept wondering why my other co-workers were leaving. It was really bizarre . . . dishes were always being broken . . . it was crazy.

In fact, for this particular worker, there was even a sense of nostalgia for those chaotic days.

> From then on it started improving, very slowly, and then when [the new supervisor] came in, then the curve went up in the last year. You wouldn't recognize it. There was excitement . . . keeping on your toes, two hours sleep and drinking coffee all the time, never a dull moment. And I do have a problem with it being so quiet [now]. [In the early days] we were making it up as we went, and we called [the supervisor] in from another program to help us. We were fairly new and needed some direction and guidance. So, one of the reasons I stayed was because she was pretty supportive, and the learning curve was all straight up.

In addition to highlighting the growing pains that were quite typical in the stories of many of the homes in this study, these observations highlight the critical role of the home supervisor in the formation and ongoing development of the living environment.

Supervising

In addition to the overall framework-setting responsibility of managers, a number of key roles and processes involved in the evolution of a group home became apparent in both the field observations and the interviews with participants. Standing out above all other factors was the home supervisor and the supervisor's role and functioning. Time and again staff and managers alike emphasized this aspect. The manager of Metro Agency stated that "the most significant person . . . in any residential program is the supervisor." A staff member at Oriole expressed his experience with supervision this way.

> If you have an unhealthy situation with the staff team, and obviously including the supervising role, you're going to get, somehow, pulled into it. You can't avoid it, in my opinion. You're going to get people who are here to do their own job, and here to do their own thing. It's hokey to say "there is no 'I' in team," but they weren't team players, and they had no interest in being team players, and a lot of that was the old supervisor didn't care what you thought, and didn't care how you wanted to do something. . . . So, obviously with that kind of non-support, you're going to get a rebellion going on, and sure enough, in fact, we got it.

The new supervisor brought a very different orientation to the role into the Oriole home.

> [The new supervisor] is the best. She would let us give our feedback. She would let us say things she didn't like; the whole thing, right? She would support us. . . . She didn't come down from some higher kind of place. I mean, the fact that she's below us, her office is lower than us [on the first floor] kind of symbolizes it. She would simply say, "Is this going to benefit the kid? Is it in his best interests? Then, we'll do it." I don't remember the other [supervisor] ever saying that.

Many more comments by staff across most of the homes corroborated these experiences of the vital role of the supervisor in ensuring the proper functioning of the staff and the home. Perhaps one brief comment from another Oriole staff member sums up the key impact of the role: "A good supervisor can create a good team, and a good team makes a good program." Indeed, the observations and conversations undertaken within this research project confirmed the significance of this influence sequence. But what makes a good supervisor?

Reducing all of the comments and observations of this study to their most basic elements, the response to the question is: "being supportively challenging." It was demonstrated many times and by numerous workers that there needs to be a balance of active support and active challenging experienced by the workers through the supervisor's words and deeds. This concept is perhaps most vividly illustrated in the words of another Oriole worker:

> The role of the supervisor is very important and ultimately affects the kids. They play an extremely important role in providing quality care to the kids in that they empower their team; they are responsible for creat-

ing a team. When [the new supervisor] came in, it was our call; she believes in us. She won't do the work for us. Whenever a question comes up, we need to talk about it. She won't rescue us; she'll challenge us. She'd call me out when she thought I wasn't doing something appropriate. I sometimes would kick the dirt like a little kid: "I hate her, I hate her." But I tell you what, damned if she wasn't right! And she didn't do the work for me, but she asked me to look at what I was doing.

Being "supportively challenging" means not simply criticizing and finding fault, as had been a common experience of supervision by many workers in this study over their residential careers. Nor does it mean simply praising and acting as a crutch for workers who are struggling to find their way, as had also been the experience of some staff members in the past. It appears that criticism without support is demoralizing, and support without criticism is debilitating. And once again, as did the Ministry manager quoted earlier, this worker made a direct connection between the functioning of a person at a high level of the organization with the program experienced by the residents on a daily basis. It was evident in this study that even committed and skilled careworkers could be undermined and become discouraged by poor supervision. On the other hand, even less skilled workers, when supported and inspired, demonstrated good-enough carework on quite a consistent basis as a result of being effectively supervised.

From the youth perspective, the coherence, reciprocity, and consistency across diverse staff provided an important sense of safety that the residents needed in order for them to be able to trust sufficiently that they could be themselves and reveal their vulnerabilities, without being subjected to rejection or further harm. All of the young people in this study were removed from their families or foster families and placed into the group homes because either their needs exceeded what could be met in more normative environments or their behaviors exceeded what could be tolerated within familial settings and required concerted attention.

Another element evident in the well-enough supervised homes was an understanding of the difference between "delegating" and "giving responsibility." In a delegating mode, the supervisor asks or expects workers to "do as they are told" or to "do it as I want you to do it." In contrast, an effective supervisor will give the responsibility to the worker to handle some task or situation, trusting that it will be handled responsibly and effectively even if not necessarily as the supervisor would have handled it. This giving of responsibility requires having trust in the staff team. In addition to challenging and supporting individual workers, the supervisor has the key role to play in leading and shaping the staff team.

Teamwork

As reiterated several times in the previous quotations, teamwork is a critically important element in the creation of a group home environment. Once again, an Oriole worker captures the significance of teamwork on the basis of her own experience over several years in the home.

> At [Oriole], there was a program description, I'm sure, but I don't know what it was. At first, it was basically just a containment house. In team, we weren't clear what we were doing as a team; just whatever personal agenda a person had. Everybody was doing their own thing. Rules changed all the time. Kids could do whatever they wanted depending on what staff was on shift. There was no real structure or expectations for the kids. It was basically just housing them. There was no sense of accomplishment; there was no system happening. We were doing regular reports, but without any goals.

Then, the new supervisor arrived, and things changed.

> [She] said: "You don't know what you are doing. I don't believe this. There are kids who have been staying here for 8 months! Let's get back to the plan here. . . . You guys are great workers; here are your strengths. Let's create a program; let's do it!" She gave us some ideas, helped us to focus on our goal which is to provide the kids with a structured, safe environment for a short period of time while they received assessment. What we recognized is that in order to assess these kids, we need to get to know them. We need to know them very quickly since they are going to be here a short period of time, where they can do well. [We need to help with their] social competence. As well, they need some support, and we do that with a structure. So, we needed to create a program that was going to highlight and show these areas in these kids so we could figure out how we can best support them. And by doing that, it gave us all ownership of the program because we made it, and we had a clear goal. We made the entire program to fit our mandate and what they expected, and what we were supposed to be doing. We had all been acknowledged for our strengths. We had all been acknowledged for the things we needed to work on, and the team grew. And it became a really tight team, and we worked *together*.

Strong parallels can be seen between the process of a supervisor supportively challenging staff members, and careworkers supportively challenging the residents. Indeed, in the next chapter, a set of interactional dynamics that have been identified over the course of this research as needing to be present at all levels of group home operation in a well-functioning home will be explored in some detail.

But what makes a good team? As has already been mentioned, a central aspect of a good team is that workers do not simply follow their own agendas but rather create a common understanding and plan for their work together. This is a developmental process, and it was apparent that the transition could be a painful and difficult one as individuals faced their limitations as well as their responsibilities towards each other and towards the residents. However, in addition to being a learning place for the workers, the team becomes a kind of safety net for the residents. It was evident that if there was a lack of clarity and consistency within the team, the residents would quickly detect the gap and push through it. As one of the youth intimated in conversation, it was not that they wanted to break through the staff's structure; quite the opposite. What the residents really wanted and needed was to find a sense of comfort and security in the staff team and to know that whatever happened, and whatever they did, the team would remain strong, united and protective. Only then could the residents let go of their own defenses and begin to trust in the adults around them, thus discovering a safe environment within which they could begin their own healing and growth processes. The strength and cohesion of staff members was thus seen as an essential ingredient in order for the developmental and therapeutic purposes of a home to be realized.

Much has also been said by the workers already quoted about the importance of creating the group home program. The meaning and significance of a program within a group home context is the next aspect of the environment to be explored.

Programming

In its briefest formulation, a program is "a set of activities organised for a purpose" (Anglin & Working Group, 1978). Thus, in a group home, the program consists of the planned activities arranged by the staff within the daily functioning of the home. Given the diverse and transitory nature of both the resident and the staff groups, there is a need to create a well-planned environment that addresses the needs of the residents, individually and collectively. There is a tendency in some workers' minds to equate the program with a plan–whether or not that plan is consistently or ever put into practice. Such a plan, while potentially a program, is not in fact a program until it is consistently implemented. Also, activities undertaken spontaneously or on an ad hoc basis do not constitute a program either. While all homes included within this study had some form of program in place, they varied considerably in their scope and density. By *scope* is meant the range of types of activities included, and by *density* is meant the amount of activity carried out within a given time period.

Whatever the level of sophistication, it was evident within this study that a program appears to serve a mediating function, in the sense that it acts as a buffer between the staff and the young residents in relation to behavioral expectations and consequences. In the words of one careworker at Oriole:

> The best thing about this house is the program runs itself. It is not us giving them consequences, telling them to follow rules . . . it's the program. When the program runs itself, it makes us be the helpers; we're not the bad guys.

At Mountainview, the setting that had the most sophisticated behavioral charting system, the staff understood the primary function of a charting system as an opportunity to engage in a focused conversation with each resident each evening.

> The chart review [happens] every evening . . . once a day we have a life-space interview called "coming to see your chart." And within that context we can review the whole day. "What are you doing? You can't let [other boys'] weaknesses go. You're building yourself up by doing that stuff. That concerns me, my friend. Because this is what I'm fearing you've learned . . . that absolute power is absolute, and when you get some of your own, you get to dump on everybody else (which is his family, I'm sure, the way he speaks)."

In the Mountainview approach, what was more important than the number of points obtained or the level achieved was the opportunity to review the young person's performance over the day and to explore what these behaviors and attitudes meant in the young person's life.

> We try to use those opportunities in a day to hook their feelings and their behavior. You have a chance at intervening and maybe changing lifestyle. When they learn to question themselves, it is a very difficult thing at first, but like a lot of treatment modalities, it invokes insight. I've seen guys have *tons* of insight. . . . Every person at work has worth. Inappropriate and appropriate communication . . . it gives tons of inroads to counseling later, as I said, in the chart review, or in a private moment when we're down in the sauna at chore time. "N., what are you doin'?" [Laughter] Informal things provided by our environment.

The young residents noticed the difference when carework staff did not badger them but rather acknowledged their own ability and responsibility to make choices. In programs where staff clarified the expectations and demonstrated confidence in the fairness and appropriateness of the program, no matter how basic or how sophisticated, it was evident that the young people tended to be less confrontational with staff and demonstrated a greater sense of responsibility for their own actions and their consequences. In homes where staff had a clear sense of implementing a program and a philosophical understanding that the residents needed to learn by making choices, there were few power or control struggles observed with the residents. As has already been noted, Parke Street, the one home with virtually no visible ongoing programming (except for a half-day work experience opportunity outside of the home for a few of the residents), experienced a full-blown riot during the period of this research, and the police had to be called in to restore order. It would seem that if staff do not create some form of program structure, the youth will organize their own forms of activity, often negative, to fill the perceived vacuum.

At the same time, programming is only one dimension of the created living environment. Carework is the term being used here to refer to the primary, ongoing developmental and therapeutic work of the care staff within a group home environment, and, thus, it is deserving of particular attention.

Carework

Many terms have been used in the literature on residential care to refer to the direct, hands-on work, and the term "care" itself has been questioned in this context. Clough (2000, pp. 60-61), for example, indicates that "care" can be taken to mean a maintaining of a dependency, whereas many clients want–and need–to exert their independence to the maximum extent possible. However, Clough also suggests that the term "care" has connotations of nurture as well as of safety, and, therefore, this study will retain this construct to describe the daily functioning of the carework staff. Carework, used in this sense, will encompass both the direct contact involvements with the residents as well as the indirect and more organizational aspects (such as report writing, making meals and driving) as well. What becomes apparent in observing the "indirect" carework activities is that they very frequently involve contact and interaction with the residents as well. Reports are sometimes of considerable interest to the residents, and several of the homes in this study made a practice of reading the draft reports to the residents as a way of discussing their progress and experiences within the home, in school, with their families, and in other activities. And rarely is a meal prepared or a resident driven without considerable banter, discussion, argument, or confidence-sharing taking place between careworkers and youth.

The process of carework is generally considered the most complex, demanding, and important aspect of residential life, and yet the literature consistently acknowledges that, paradoxically, it is the least respected, valued, and understood element in the provision of residential care (Clough, 2000, p. 36). While this research did not attempt to explore the reasons for such a state of affairs, it seems plausible that the social devaluing of the staff in group homes is associated with the societal devaluing of their residents. There appears to be a general perception amongst members of the public and evidenced in conversations with many of the youth themselves that the residents of group homes must have done something wrong to be there. There is a lack of appreciation for the fact that the large majority of the residents of child protection group homes, such as those in this study sample, have been placed there due to the neglectful or abusive behavior of their parents. Even in instances where the residents have histories of such antisocial or illegal behaviors as violence, theft, or substance abuse, often these can be understood as direct or indirect reactions of exposure to personal experiences of neglect and abuse. The fact that young people living in other residential establishments such as elite boarding schools, as well as the staff that supervise them, are not subjected to such negative judgements indicates that it is not residential placement or residential living per se that is stigmatized (Clough, 2000, pp. 9-10).

Given the traumatic backgrounds of the residents in the group homes studied, the carework function is seen as involving two intertwined purposes: a developmental purpose and a therapeutic purpose. On the basis of discussions with many of the youths in care and their careworkers, it was evident that every one of the residents and recent graduates had indeed experienced traumatic events in their lives, with removal from their family home and placement in an extrafamilial home being but one of the more recent incidents. Further, as a result of various traumas, every youth placed in these homes was experiencing deep-seated and often acute distress. In the next chapter, the crucial significance of this fact for both an adequate understanding of these homes and of the demands of practice within them will be examined.

The creation of a group home has been seen to involve physical and structural elements as well as process elements. The physical and structural elements included the physical setting, the residents, and the staff, while the process elements included contracting (with the Ministry), managing, supervising, teamwork, programming, and carework. It was apparent in the study that these elements, all characteristics of an artificial, planned environment, required careful crafting and shaping. It is evident that these elements represent very significant differences between a group home and either a foster or biological family home. Further, seven characteristics further differentiating these two types of environments were uncovered from an analysis of the residents' experiences over the course of this study, and these will now be explored.

FAMILIAL VERSUS EXTRAFAMILIAL LIVING ENVIRONMENTS

One of the persistent questions in the field of residential care is how to decide whether to place a young person in foster care or in group home care.

Some individuals and jurisdictions have even expressed the view that group homes are a form of institution, and that no young person should ever have to reside in a group home setting (Boone, 1999; Cliffe & Berridge, 1992). As a form of extrafamilial care, group homes have come into question in the attack mounted against residential care in general over the past several decades (Gottesman, 1994, pp. 2-9).

However, in the words of one young resident at Yellowdale, there are times when some young people do "really, really need" a group home. Residents and former residents in this study who believed that their experiences in group homes had been largely beneficial identified a number of common preferred characteristics and in several instances explicitly contrasted these to some of their negative experiences in foster homes. It is important to recognize that a number of the youth respondents also had very positive foster home experiences. What this section is exploring are aspects of the group homes in this sample that were experienced by some residents to be positive and preferred in their experience, at a particular stage in their life and "career in care" (Brown, Bullock, Hobson & Little, 1998, p. 3). Also reflected in this discussion are some of the perceptions and observations of careworkers and supervisory staff members that speak to the benefits and advantages of group homes for addressing certain needs of youth.

The seven characteristics of group home environments that have emerged over the course of the study are presented in Table 3. Each characteristic will now be briefly discussed along with an examination of its potential implications for the care and development of the group home residents. Once again, it is important to keep in mind that this analysis is not implying that foster homes are not suitable placements for many young people in care. Quite to the contrary, it would appear that a foster family is a preferred placement for many young people, and even the majority of young people. However, it is equally evident that for some young people, at certain times in their lives, a group home may be the preferred setting.

Staff-Youth Relationships

As the Pioneer Place supervisor stated, "You can't replace that biological bond (to family), and we can't compete with it. I'd rather put more effort on working together, on how (the youth and parents) see each other. . . ." The findings of this study strongly challenge the notion that group homes should strive to be surrogate families. Sometimes when foster placements are not acceptable or helpful for a youth, it is because they experience a sense of betrayal when they are faced with the expectation to "treat strangers as family." The reality can be, as one girl said, "I feel I'm just some intruder in someone's house." An-

TABLE 3. Comparison of Children's Living Environments

Characteristics	Parent Home	Foster Home	Staffed Group Home	Institution
Relationships	biological or adoptive family	foster family	carework staff and non-related peers	carework staff and other professionals and peers
Physical Setting	parent home	parent home	agency house in community	government facility
Number of People (Carers & Youth)	2 to 5+	2 to 5+	15+	50 to 100+
Time Element (Carers)	full-time, lifelong	full-time, some respite	shift work (8, 12, 24, 48 or 72 hours)	shift work–normally 8 hours
Style of Care	intimate	informal to intimate	semi-formal; paraprofessional	formal; professional
Intensity of Care/ Treatment	familial care	familial care (plus structure)	staff care, elements of therapeutic care	intensive care, custody, and/or treatment
Supervision of Carers	none	minimal and indirect	direct and ongoing	direct and ongoing

other young group home resident said, "I don't need a family; I already have a family!"

Several young people expressed the feeling that they had to "behave themselves" when in foster care to the degree that they did not feel that they could really be themselves and begin to address the issues that led them to be placed there in the first place. However, even when a foster placement did not ultimately work out, there were often positive memories as well. It needs to be kept in mind that the young people in this study ranged in age from 10 years to 18 years, and that the desire for, appreciation of, and ability to relate to a surrogate family may be much more evident with younger children in care.

Physical Setting

Whereas a group home is usually owned by an agency, or in some cases the provincial government, a foster home is rented or owned by the foster parents. The furnishings, personal belongings, and the house itself represent a significant emotional as well as financial investment for the parents and other family members. To damage or treat with disrespect someone's valued and sentimental belongings is to inflict, to a greater or lesser degree, both an emotional hurt and a financial burden upon their owner. As the manager of the Valley Agency observed, "Parents cannot accept a young person doing damage to their home; it's beyond the limits they can tolerate."

There is also an issue of safety for both the parents and youth and any children or other relatives living in the foster home. Some of the youth in this study who enjoyed living in foster care when things were going well knew at the same time that there were occasions when they were unable to control their outbursts of anger and rage and realized themselves on these occasions that they were unable to deal with their psychological and emotional problems adequately within a family home setting. In one situation in this study, a 13-year-old boy and former group home resident asked to be temporarily removed from his foster home for a two-month period and replaced in the group home that he had left a year or so before. In his words:

> I like being [at the foster home]. I love being here. It's just at the time I was going through some pretty crazy stuff, and I knew I was going to blow it if I stayed here much longer. . . . I needed a place where I was going to go off the wall, and I wasn't going to burn any bridges. I needed to be somewhere where I could be where I wasn't going to hurt anyone, lash out at the wrong people, which I did there [i.e., at the group home], but it wasn't too bad. . . .

In the eyes of the foster parent, this was a decision she could understand and support as well:

> Yup, he needed a 24-hour place for him. And his temper was getting really violent: smashing rooms, smashing walls . . . we couldn't pinpoint his anger. His safety was the biggest issue, and I just couldn't provide enough safety for him. In going to [the group home], there is more staff there, he is supervised all the time. It was the best thing for him.

In a well-functioning group home, a young person knows that the staff will be able to accept more challenging behavior, and can offer a safer environment while he or she can, in the words of another former group home resident, "work out a lot of my problems."

Number of People in the Household

Some young people are only too ready to trade what they experience as a stifling level of intimacy in a foster home for the variety of possible relationships and role models that they can experience in a group home setting. As one youth commented:

> I never had a favorite staff. Overall they were pretty neat people. One lady, she was a leading horse trainer in Canada, and [another staff] climbed Canada's highest mountain, and stuff. They were pretty interesting people to me.

While foster parents can also offer impressive life experiences and serve as powerful role models, there are only one or two of them, and there is more pressure on these relationships to "click" than with a range of full-time, part-time, and relief staff found in a group home situation. While adult relationships are often experienced as very important for youth in care, the young people in this study who were going through intense personal struggles and were at their least likeable, sometimes expressed appreciation for caring relationships that came without the expectation of close or ongoing intimacy. Some foster parents understand their roles as being surrogate parents rather than as adult carers within a family environment, even to the point of wanting the young person to fulfill the parent's needs to be treated as "mum and dad." The young people who had experienced group home care as therapeutic had generally felt stifled by such expectations when in foster care.

Time Element (of Carers On-Site)

While it was evident in this study that the longer staff shifts (e.g., three or four days straight) were often preferred by the youth to the eight- or twelve-hour shifts, the residents also realized that the staff needed a break to refresh themselves if they were going to be able to work effectively with them. Staff were typically very clear about the advantages of regular and frequent breaks given the demanding needs and behaviors of some of the residents, but so were some of the resident youth. One resident eloquently acknowledged the demands that he knew his behavior placed on residential staff: "I knew the staff got changed every four days, and that would be enough time for them to have a break, and calm down, and come back to work and deal with me."

For foster parents, respite tends to be quite brief and infrequent, when it happens at all, and the youth noticed and could speak to the difference it made for the atmosphere that they experienced. The image of a foster home setting as an "emotional hothouse" would be an apt characterisation of some youth's experiences. In a group home, to continue the image, the air may get quite heavy and steamy, but the walls are not made with so much glass and there are many more gardeners to call upon when needed.

Style of Care

While the intimate and familial aspects of foster care can be an important source of nurturing and offer a sense of belonging for many young people, for those who are suffering through the deep-seated effects of trauma and who have difficulty controlling their "acting out" or "pain-based behavior," the less intimate and more youth-centered attention of staff members may make the difference between an experience of personal change and yet another failure experience (i.e., a foster home breakdown). As one young group home resident observed, "In a foster home I am expected to fit in; here, they work to fit in with me."

One of the staff members at Dogwood observed:

> Having two full-time staff on plus a supervisor allows you to stay on top of things. . . . There is just so much more support here, and that's what we're structured to do. There are no other things we need to look after. We don't need to look after our private life, because it's not here!

And a careworker at Yellowdale said, "We are not trying to look after our own children [in the group home] . . . and we have nothing else to do here but grow [together]."

Intensity of Care/Treatment

The well-functioning group homes in this study were continually seeking to provide therapeutic care and a consistency of structure and expectations with an intensity that is virtually impossible to maintain in a family or foster family setting. A careworker at Yellowdale commented:

> I think that being here helps them [i.e., the youth residents] to manage themselves instead of them learning to *act* appropriately in other settings. I think that one of the strongest benefits is that they can learn to make choices that are going to work, instead of just sort of having a façade. And I think the long-term benefits and the day-to-day benefits are learning what's appropriate and what's not appropriate, and having the steady input from the staff every day for their whole placement I really think helps them to change those behaviors.

Another Yellowdale careworker said, "Here there is stability in consistency of expectations, consistency of rules, consistency in response to behaviors . . . and reactions." A foster parent for one of the former Yellowdale residents concurred: "Well, one of the things I think is excellent [at Yellowdale] is that when he acts out, they have one staff who can go off just with him, where I can't. . . . They can enforce the rules better than I can. I can push it to a point, but when a kid starts harming himself, then I can't [deal with that]."

The fact is that the intensity of care and treatment offered in a well-functioning staffed home cannot be matched in most foster homes, and many young people in this study indicated that they required such intensity of interaction for a significant period of time while they struggled with their problems and the pain and anger associated with them. They realized that their pain-based outbursts seriously interfered with their ability to interact with others and, on occasion, to live safely with themselves.

Supervision of Carers

In a foster home setting, the parents are on their own except for occasional consultations and perhaps a few visits per year from a Ministry resource worker. Even the current standard (not often met in practice) that calls for monthly visits allows for monitoring and occasional support rather than close supervision. Typically, in a well-functioning group home situation, there is quite close and direct supervision and what can be termed "co-vision" by a co-worker working on the same shift. In the homes studied, most of the supervisors were more seasoned staff whose role it was to ensure that their colleagues were functioning appropriately, both in the moment and over time. As a careworker observed in an earlier quotation, "She (the supervisor) won't rescue us, she'll challenge us. I always know that she's there." Indeed, attentive and competent supervision emerged as one of the core and essential elements contributing to a well-functioning group home.

If staff members "lose it," become overwhelmed, or conduct themselves inappropriately in a staffed and well-supervised group home, another staff member or supervisor will likely become aware of it and can take appropriate action. Over the course of this study, there were several instances of co-workers or supervisors intervening on behalf of a young person in care to counterbalance or correct some inappropriate behavior on the part of another staff member. In one instance, a worker on a shift reported an incident of aggressive physical behavior by her co-worker that was investigated by both the agency and the Ministry resulting in the resignation of the staff member in question.

In this study, it was apparent that effective supervision allowed for an intensity of interaction and offered some protection against abusive or excessive reactions that could and did occur in such a "pressure cooker" environment. In a foster home, there may be no one in a position pick up on the foster parent's inappropriate behavior or to know when and how to provide direction when a foster parent is feeling stuck or frustrated.

SUMMARY

Seven characteristics that serve to differentiate group homes from foster homes emerged from conversations with youth residents, former youth residents, careworkers, supervisors, and foster parents. This brief analysis serves to demonstrate that some of the perceived limitations of group homes in relation to foster family care are actually some of their very strengths for the segment of the child population that requires what group homes have to offer.

What well-functioning group homes can offer is an intense, supervised, staffed, structured, less emotionally charged and more consistently responsive environment for promoting the personal growth and development of youth who require such intensive care and support. If a service is to be utilized, then we need to know how, when, and for whom it can best be used and value it as a positive choice in these circumstances. A service that is not valued or that is considered always to be an unsatisfactory or second-rate option will inevitably deteriorate and will ultimately reflect these self-fulfilling expectations. The findings of this study suggest that group homes need to be appreciated for their strengths as extrafamilial developmental and therapeutic environments and ought not to be denigrated for not being "natural" or "real" families.

Chapter 6
Responding to Pain and Pain-Based Behavior: The Major Challenge for Staff

For most of us . . . childhood feelings are manageable and healthy, even though they may cause us considerable pain and confusion at the time: but for children who have experienced the trauma of rejection, neglect, or abuse, their inner world is often in a greater turmoil than the "real" world around them. . . . The worker who attempts to achieve communication with the child's inner world is therefore operating in highly sensitive territory; here, timing, patience and an ability to demonstrate real empathy are essential.

–Adrian Ward and Linnet McMahon (1998, pp. 13-14)

On one of the trips to visit the three homes of the Valley Agency in the final months of the study, a residential worker was being interviewed in a local restaurant over lunch. She had worked in a number of residential programs over a period of eight years, but she was frank in her admission that she did not see her work as more than a job: "I am committed to the job while I am doing it, but not as a career." She had worked in all three of the Valley Agency homes involved in the study as well as a home that had recently undergone substantial redesign. Early in the conversation she said:

> It was a place for little kids to be. They came in with a lot of hurt and anger, and the teenagers do as well, and you are dealing with a lot of repercussions of their anger, so there's little opportunity to get into the head of the child and make a difference with their emotions.

[Haworth co-indexing entry note]: "Responding to Pain and Pain-Based Behavior: The Major Challenge for Staff." Anglin, James P. Co-published simultaneously in *Child & Youth Services* (The Haworth Press, Inc.) Vol. 24, No. 1/2, 2002, pp. 107-121; and: *Pain, Normality, and the Struggle for Congruence: Reinterpreting Residential Care for Children and Youth* (James P. Anglin) The Haworth Press, Inc., 2002, pp. 107-121. Single or multiple copies of this article are available for a fee from The Haworth Document Delivery Service [1-800-HAWORTH, 9:00 a.m. - 5:00 p.m. (EST). E-mail address: docdelivery@haworthpress.com].

http://www.haworthpress.com/store/product.asp?sku=J024
10.1300/J024v24n01_07

A little later in the conversation, she added:

> The staff was always there. But there was so much time taken up in be-
> haviors, and dealing with behavior, and trying to have the home run
> smoothly. In other words, "let's make our beds," "let's go to school,"
> "let's get our homework done," "let's have our supper," "let's all clean
> up." There was so much time needing to be involved in having it all run
> smoothly, that even though staff were always there, for a discussion, and
> "how are you feeling about this," "what's happening," "talk to me about
> it"–and a lot of that happened–it wasn't enough to make an impact on be-
> havior change.

This description of the anger and hurt of the young people in some of the
homes being studied, the "repercussions" of this hurt and anger, and the busyness of the daily life of staff and residents powerfully conveys a common reality of group home life observed in this study. Despite this ongoing interaction,
discussion or conversation–either between the staff and the residents or even
amongst the staff members themselves–was seldom evident concerning the
underlying hurt that was being experienced and carried by these young people.

The many activities of daily life seemed to disguise and cover over this
ever-present and deep-seated pain to the point where one wondered if this
"cover up" was an intentional strategy of avoidance. From time to time, what
staff variously called "outbursts," "explosions," or "acting out" on the part of
residents would occur in the homes, and while it appeared to an observer that
the reaction evidenced inner turmoil and pain, seldom did careworkers acknowledge or respond sensitively to the inner world of the child. Often, a staff
member would react to such behavior by making verbal demands of a controlling nature (e.g., "Get a grip on yourself!" or "Watch your language now!") or
giving a warning of possible consequences in terms of lost points, time-out, or
withdrawal of privileges.

It is not uncommon in child and youth work and child care literature to see
the core task of care being referred to as "behavior management" (Shostack,
1997, p. 132) or even as "controlling children's behavior" (Millham et al.,
1981, p. 17). One experienced supervisor articulated his understanding of this
aspect as follows:

> Make no mistake about it . . . this is residential care and these children are
> from a very different social group. And the bottom line is large, compe-
> tent people who can control. Even after all that nice stuff I've said about
> therapy and taking your therapy to another level, it's the bottom line al-
> ways, for the community, and for the agency. . . . If there is no control,
> there is no listening. In this residential work, we need to control. The

mistake, I guess, is in not figuring out that the staff don't have to do all the control. The kids can do a lot for themselves. The kids can really do a lot of that for each other. . . . So, I say, in the long run residential care is control, the place has to be controlled. If it goes out of control, there's going to be no getting better, if everybody has gotten out of control.

Ironically, the home supervised by this supervisor had, a few weeks before this interview, been subjected to a riot by the residents. In this incident, residents restricted staff members to the office, broke windows, emptied cupboards, and generally "trashed" the house to the point that the police had to be called to restore order. While other homes in the study had experienced individual residents losing control, this was the only incident of an entire home going out of control that came to the researcher's attention over the course of this study. It would appear on the basis of observations in this study that a philosophy of staff control may tend to breed aggressive reactions, whereas acknowledging each youth's freedom of choice and encouraging them to make good choices tends to limit the incidence of such explosive behavior.

As the study progressed, and the researcher began to experience more fully the painful realities just below the "superficial layer" of busyness, the half-forgotten titles of two books came to mind. One book by Leonard Davis (1987) about the experiences of young people in care was entitled *Rivers of Pain, Bridges of Hope*. The second, about youth in the child welfare system written by a former youth-in-care, was called *Pain . . . lots of pain* (Raychaba, 1993). Upon reviewing the field notes, the interview transcripts, and reflecting back over experiences in the homes with youth, careworkers, parents and supervisors, it became increasingly evident that the swirl of often angry behaviors and the ongoing "repercussions" of staff reactions were fundamentally rooted in the generally under-acknowledged and largely unaddressed psychoemotional pain of the residents.

The children and adolescents who came into the group settings participating in this study had been removed from abusive, neglectful, or overwhelming personal situations, and they came into substitute care with deep-seated and typically long-standing pain. This pain sometimes had physical manifestations, such as self-mutilation, but the predominant pain was not physical but psychoemotional. Interviews revealed that the painful experiences of the residents that could erupt into outbursts and explosions or lead to a wall of protectiveness aimed towards all adults, had resulted from various combinations of the following: grief at losses and abandonment; persistent anxiety about themselves and their situation; fear of or even terror about a disintegrating present and a hopeless future; depression and dispiritedness at a lack of meaning or sense of purpose in their lives; and what could be termed "psychoemotional paralysis," or a state of numbness and withdrawal from the people and world around them.

A study by McCann and James (1996) of the prevalence and types of psychiatric disorder among adolescents in the care system in Oxfordshire, England, revealed that 96% of the adolescents in residential units and 57% in foster care had psychiatric disorders (p. 1529). Polnay and Ward (2000) also report that the young people "who come into the system are among the most vulnerable children in our society. They have a higher level of health, mental health, and health promotion needs than others of the same age" (p. 661). While no comparable study has been published on the Canadian care system, the findings of this study would suggest a similar profile of adolescents in care.

With such chronic psychoemotional pain being carried within, these young people become veritable time-bombs for those attempting to relate or work with them. It is as if there are invisible triggers attached to internalized traumas that can set off an explosion without a moment's notice, and sometimes attached with slow-burning fuses that can be lit unknowingly and that will result in a detonation some time later if the tell-tale smoldering signs are not detected and respected. Workers in the better functioning homes tended to respond by interpreting the behavior and responding sensitively rather than by immediately imposing external controls. At the same time, several of the well-functioning homes in the study bore evidence of such outbursts through holes in the walls, broken windows, and damaged furniture and appliances. On one visit, the manager at Yellowdale greeted the researcher with fresh wall-board filler on his hands and in his hair, in the midst of doing some major repair work after a difficult weekend. Responding with understanding and respect does not necessarily prevent such outbursts, but it can increase the likelihood that they can be turned into learning opportunities for the youth.

A number of words could have been used to describe the internal aspect of the lived experience of youth in group home care such as "stress," "distress" or, the most common term in the current literature, "troubled." A number of prominent texts in the child and youth care field use the latter term in titles such as *Re-Educating Troubled Youth* (Brendtro & Ness, 1983), *Caring for Troubled Children* (Whittaker, 1979), *Working with Troubled Children* (Savicki & Brown, 1985), and *The Troubled and Troubling Child* (Hobbs, 1982). However, as has already been mentioned, some of the most powerful writing about the experiences of youth in care by careworkers and by former youth in care themselves explicitly uses the word "pain" (Davis, 1987; Raychaba, 1993). Therefore, it seems most appropriate and accurate to use this term in order not to risk glossing over the stark and deeply painful reality of the lived experience of these young people.

In this study, according to the testimony of youth themselves and their care-workers, *every young person without exception* who was living in the homes or who was interviewed as a former resident had experienced deep and pervasive psychoemotional pain at the time of coming into the group programs and throughout their time in residence. It needs to be remembered that these were group care settings within the child protection domain, with the exception of one that accommodated male young offenders. While the situation may be somewhat different for children and youth entering group care facilities catering to young people with developmental disabilities or some other set of needs, it would be reasonable to assume that the reality of separation from one's family of origin is in itself likely to be a source of significant psychoemotional pain.

The formal interviews with young people in this study, as well as informal discussions with former youth in care outside of this study, suggest that the manner and degree to which this pain is responded to is one of the key indicators of the quality of care in a residence as experienced by the youth. Those young people who had made successful transitions out of group home care back into their family home, foster care, or independent living had internalized self-awareness and self-management skills as a means of dealing with the underlying and ever-present psychoemotional pain and the potential for pain-based behavior. The literature on adult survivors of childhood trauma suggests that the pain may never fully "disappear," but being able to cope with it in a manner that will allow for the achievement of a sense of normality requires that the pain be named, owned, understood in its developmental context, and placed within a personal story that can lead to a desired future. The stories of the former group home residents interviewed demonstrated that well-enough functioning programs could assist in at least launching this process. Outcomes such as improved school attendance, steady employment, more realistic and sustainable relations with family members, and successful independent living appeared to be closely linked to an acceptance of the past, a sense of hope for the future, and the development of self-management skills. In many cases, the youth could trace key moments in this learning process back to moments and relationships experienced in the group home settings.

The term "pain-based behavior" is an abbreviated way of saying "behavior, either of an 'acting out' or withdrawn nature that is triggered by the reexperiencing of psychoemotional pain." The existence of this residue of unresolved past traumas makes interactions with youth in such pain often unpredictable and volatile. Further, staff themselves can have their own unaddressed pain triggered by the presence of pain experiences in the youth or the "acting out" behavior of youth, resulting in pain-based behavior being exhibited by staff themselves. Thus, pain-based behavior is not a property of just the young people in care alone.

THE PERSONAL PAIN-BASED CHALLENGES OF STAFF

Interviews undertaken in this study suggest that a significant number of staff are attracted to this form of work with the motivation of "making things better" for youth who have experienced the kind of pain and trauma that the staff themselves have experienced. In this sample, approximately half of the staff interviewed indicated a personally painful childhood background. As Ward and McMahon (1998) indicate in the opening quote at the start of this chapter, all children experience a degree of pain and confusion over the course of their development. However, if this pain is the result of abuse, rejection, or neglect, its lingering effects will almost inevitably be reawakened or magnified when similar experiences are encountered in the intense interaction with youth that characterizes group home life and work. This fact highlights the critical importance of self-awareness and self-development training in the preparation of careworkers and the necessity of effective ongoing supervision of practice, especially in relation to worker "anxiety" (pain-based fear).

Even as a researcher visiting the homes, the author experienced considerable anxiety in the face of the often overwhelming pain and pain-based behavior exhibited by the residents. Leaving the group home, it often took a few hours for the experience of varying degrees of anger and frustration at what these young people had experienced—and continued to experience—to dissipate. On several occasions, the researcher awakened in the night, "troubled" by what had been experienced the day or evening before. However, while it was apparent to the researcher that being continually exposed to such deep and pervasive pain took a significant personal toll, many of the workers seemed to be relatively unaffected by even very much more intense exposure. When asked about the ongoing presence of pain amongst all of the young residents, one of the Oak Lane manager/supervisors responded:

> I don't know if we couldn't put into words that we saw the pain and this is how we were dealing with it. You know, I think you're right on. I think that that's [i.e., pain] probably exactly what was there.... We focused on helping [the residents] to see another side of life, because I think we were pretty clear that they would continue to be exposed to pain in many aspects of their life and we wanted to give them, I guess, a bit of hope, and learn to relax and learn to enjoy . . . but I think you are absolutely right, that the underlying pathology is they are in pain. We were almost giving

them a suit of armor, in a sense, and some tools of their own to fall back on, in reserve, to deal with some of these situations. . . .

The second manager/supervisor added:

> Learning to have some good times with their parents, even if they are not able to live at home. I do think that some staff do become consumed with that pain, and it's not that you end up not recognizing it. . . . I know for the first year I went home with a lot of that, personally. . . . The experience is an eye-opener, and you have to learn to deal with it. And if you can't, you really can't work effectively, for yourself or the kids. . . .
>
> You become really consumed with it and wanting to protect kids from having that pain. That's the first instinct, and then I think you gradually move into trying to help them deal with it themselves instead of protecting them from everything. . . . I think that there is a high level of anxiety at a lot of places, and I think a lot of that is about the chaos factor and the unpredictability.

The data gathered in this study also indicate that the preparation of care-workers continues to be a highly problematic area in staffed group home work. It is a disturbing fact that those who have the most complex and demanding role in the care and treatment of traumatized children have the least and, in many cases, no specific training for the work. This means that many workers are being hired to work in the midst of this "river of pain" without having engaged in a process to identify, understand, and come to terms with the unresolved trauma and pain in their own backgrounds, leaving them vulnerable to defensive reactions towards the youth when the youth's pain emerges in a variety of often challenging ways.

While just over half of the staff interviewed in the course of this research had a college diploma or a university degree, many of the qualifications were not in the human services. Further, by their own admission, most credentialed and uncredentialed workers had received inadequate and, in many cases, no preparation for either working with challenging young people or in a residential setting before being hired to work for the first time in residential care. A few staff had obtained experience in working with young people in correctional facilties before being hired to work in the group homes, but such a background was generally considered by supervisors and co-workers as something that had to be unlearned and tended to be a problem rather than an asset in a group home setting.

Given the severity of the difficulties encountered by the young residents in their daily lives and the depth and pervasiveness of their psychoemotional pain, it seems imprudent at best, and negligent at worst, to place inexperienced and untrained staff in such a demanding and complex situation. Further, it cannot be in the resident children's best interests to be exposed to ineffective or repressive staff reactions to the residents' painful attempts to take action, however misguided, within their often incomprehensible and frightening situations.

SUPERVISION AND WORKER ANXIETY (PAIN-BASED FEAR)

As has been discussed earlier, it became evident over the course of this research that one of the most critical factors differentiating a well-enough functioning group home from a seriously struggling or poor one, especially given the general inadequacy of staff preparation, is the quality of supervision. The majority of homes in this study demonstrated that effective supervision was able to create, over time, a well-enough functioning team that could ensure a generally positive home experience for youth. In turn, such a home experience was seen to assist the residents to develop skills for self-managing their own experiences and behavior.

On the basis of the experiences related by careworkers and supervisors, it appears that a period of between one to two years is required to mentor a predominantly stable staff group into a well-enough functioning carework team. Given the rate of staff turnover in group homes generally, the task of supervision becomes one of maintaining a well-enough functioning team while continually hiring, orienting and incorporating new staff members.

By "well-enough functioning" in this context is meant a group home environment that is responsive rather than reactive, influencing rather than imposing controls, challenging by offering choices, demonstrating skill in reading young people's behavior accurately, and doing things *with* rather than *to* youth. These processes, noted in this study for their suitability and effectiveness in addressing potentially explosive and destructive situations, are characteristic of well-enough functioning homes and will now be examined in relation to the overall theme of congruence in service of the children's best interests.

Being Responsive versus Reactive

An experienced worker at the Parke Street home noted:

> Don't give the kids something to react to. Kids have a lot of anger bottled up in them, and when you are doing that, they're reliving it. It's not you any more; they're reliving that and they'll come out at you. Then you are charging [i.e., with a legal charge of assault] the kid for what you initiated. Staff have a whole lot to do with how kids react.

The reciprocity of these interactions is highlighted in this statement by a seasoned careworker. Less experienced or less trained staff would sometimes make statements like: "He blew up for no reason," or "I don't know what happened, he just flipped out." The difference between *reacting* and *responding* to behavior emerged as a critically important distinction in this study. A worker with just over a year of residential experience working in the Yellowdale home said, "I think I had it in my head, but to actually put it into action took some work, and learning some new reactions . . . or 'not reactions'! . . . We sat down and sort of talked about, okay, how are we going to respond to these needs, and what's that going to look like?"

To *react* is to act on the basis of some inner motive: some feeling, emotion, desire, or physiological need in the person reacting that provides the impulse to act. To *respond* is to act on the basis of intent: some aim, plan, or a state of mind that is fastened on some purpose relating to the person being responded to rather than on a need of the reactor. On the basis of the observations and conversations in this study, the ability of workers to make this critical distinction in practice (even if they did not or could not readily verbalize it) appeared to be one of the key factors differentiating more effective workers and homes from less effective ones.

The interactions that occurred between staff who responded rather than reacted to young people tended to be sensitive, respectful, and dialogical. An example would be the following response overheard at Thunderbird: "[Sam], are you sticking to the plan we agreed to this morning right now?" An example of a reactive, and thus insensitive, disrespectful, and unilateral comment by a staff member to a resident at Pioneer Place was, "Knock it off, [Rav], you're pissing me off!"

Thus, the more responsive programs and workers could be characterized as working largely from an appeal to the youth's inner sense of responsibility for their own behavior (i.e., adopting an influencing approach) rather than from an imposition of external demands, generally accompanied by some form of explicit or implicit physical or psychological coercion (i.e., adopting a control approach).

The Use of Influence versus Control

As noted earlier, the supervisor of Parke Street espoused an attitude of control, and ironically his program was subject to the most out-of-control incident by residents experienced over the course of the entire study. His position was, "Make no mistake about it . . . this is residential care . . . and the bottom line is large competent people who can control."

This supervisor was well-versed in therapeutic models and approaches and was quite eloquent in exploring the dynamics of change involving both youth in care and their careworkers. However, the "bottom line" for him was the ability to control, and the male staff members at Parke Street were indeed "large," if not at that time demonstrating a high level of competence. Ironically, many of the male staff in other homes who encountered much less confrontation and violence from equally challenging residents were not physically large. They approached the youth with more warmth, respect, and humor while maintaining a sense of firmness and expectation that the residents would adhere to the rules and agreements made within the home.

At this point, a distinction needs to be made between "maintaining a sense of order" and "maintaining control." There was a keen awareness on the part of all supervisors and managers that one needed to maintain a sense of order and structure within which the residents could function and develop more independence. One of the approaches observed in several settings was framed by some of the Mountainview staff members as "challenge by choice."

Challenge by Choice (or "Challenging You to Challenge Yourself")

The manager of the Metro Agency had worked for many years as a frontline child and youth worker and a supervisor in residential settings, and she emphasized to her staff the importance of influencing through expectation while allowing the young people choice. As one of the workers at Oriole articulated this orientation:

> You have to have a standard to draw from. [The manager] said, when you speak with kids you have to have expectation in your voice. I've always carried that with me. "When do you think you'll have your room cleaned?"

In contrast, a controlling approach would be a variation on "Clean up your room right now, or else. . . !" A non-controlling approach without a sense of expectation tends to be too open-ended and hesitant in its phrasing, such as: "Are you going to clean up your room?" Such an open-ended question, while implying choice, invites a negative response, especially in the context of a group home setting.

The staff and supervisors in several of the group home programs articulated a similar way of placing responsibility on the residents for their behavior. One Oriole careworker said, "Our supervisor talks like a Dutch Uncle about making good choices. A resident will say, 'But you don't know what I've been through!' and she'll respond, 'Yeah, but I do know you can make good choices.'"

In the words of another worker at Oriole: "I don't believe people are bad. People can make bad choices." One careworker described the Yellowdale home's philosophy of change as follows:

> My idea of what we do here is help these guys to make choices, and learn how those choices affect them . . . choices around how to manage behavior, anger, whatever their issue may be. . . . I look at it as we are not necessarily here to fix them, but to help them to work through what they need to work through and sort of fix themselves . . . and learn, and always have the opportunity to make choices that are best for them. And be able to make the wrong choices that may not work, but to get to experience that without destroying family relationships. There's an unconditionalness here that, I think, really helps them to practice all sorts of different behaviors without worrying whether or not someone is going to love them, and you know, all the other issues that can go on . . . that are important at home.

The notion of letting young people make choices, helping them to learn what good choices are, and supporting them to make better choices appeared to be one of the key differentiating characteristics between well-functioning homes and poorly-functioning homes in this study. The two settings that demonstrated ongoing difficulties with maintaining a positive atmosphere and a positive team approach within the house were both dominated by staff who demonstrated reluctance to allow the residents to make choices. In Pioneer Place, it appeared that the staff did not understand how to provide structure and expectations without exerting external and coercive control. At Parke Street, it seemed that the staff had lost much of their enthusiasm for their work and had largely retreated to the office leaving the youth without the engagement of adults who were communicating expectations and offering structured choices. In this latter instance, while the knowledge seemed to be there, the will to put it into practice was not.

Residents themselves often noted whether workers, individually or collectively, were always "nagging" them to do the right things or whether they allowed them to make their own choices. The youth did not believe that nagging or fussing about what they were going to do or not do was at all effective in either making the home run more smoothly or helping them to improve their behavior. They seemed surprised that some staff had not yet appeared to have learned that basic lesson.

One incident of mildly abusive physical behavior by a staff member that came to the researcher's attention during this study (and which was properly and thoroughly investigated by the agency and the Ministry, resulting in the resignation of the worker) involved a male worker grabbing a physically small resident by the neck and pushing him out of the staff office. The youth was not "challenged by choice" and given an expectation by the worker with the choice made clear and then left to make the choice. There were no safety issues involved, and there was no reason to be at all aggressive unless the interaction was being interpreted by the worker as a power struggle to be won. The incident appeared to be a reaction (rather than a response) by a relatively new and not fully competent staff member. The co-worker on shift with him was also quite new, but she responded appropriately by informing the home supervisor immediately by telephone. The resident was then taken to the hospital for examination to ensure that no physical damage was done. The resident was more emotionally hurt than physically, and the incident was seen by the home supervisor as a serious breach of trust that demonstrated significant shortcomings in the worker's approach to his responsibilities. As a result of this incident, the staff member resigned, and the resident youth had to be supported by other staff to reestablish a feeling of being safe within the home.

However, even settings that embraced the importance of residents' rights to make choices within the staff expectations and program structure were not averse to using other indirect forms of influence. For example, the Dogwood supervisor referred to "having the police drop by occasionally when they have time (as) part of the control thing for the kid." Dogwood is a program for very challenging youth who generally have mental health problems, have been in conflict with the law, as well as experiencing frequent violence and abuse in their upbringing. The youth justice system, including police and probation officers, provide the backup control that allows the home to function in an open fashion without depending upon physically intimidating staff members. Despite the difficult and sometimes aggressive resident population, at Dogwood the male staff members are neither large nor intimidating and exhibit a "challenge by choice" orientation.

Most of the settings were able to produce written program philosophies that served as a guideline for practice. However, most staff indicated that they either had not seen this material or had forgotten exactly what it said. It was apparent that the home supervisor's understanding of the care process and philosophy and their process of communicating it had the most significant impact on the nature of the carework overall within the home. One aspect of the carework process that proved significant in maintaining a responsive and influencing approach was the ability of workers to "read young people's behavior."

Reading Young People's Behavior

A new careworker who had been on staff at Oriole for less than a year spoke admiringly of the abilities of a co-worker and proudly of his own developing abilities:

He's good at reading kids, where they're at and how they're doing. I've learned to read kids a lot better since I started here. I'm picking up on little things, not only on how the kid is here, but also from phone conversations with parents, etcetera. I'm getting a good feel for how they're spending their time away from here. I guess it's the private detective in me: "What is going on?" I just love it! I have been making some pretty correct calls in the past month or two; it's just a feeling I have.

When workers refer to someone as being good at reading behavior, they are indicating that the worker can look behind the behavior and know where that behavior is coming from in terms of motive, intent, and context.

When a child acts from a motive, the child is reacting to some inner impulse, feeling, or emotion and is not likely thinking about the impact of the action. However, young people sometimes act with intent to have a certain impact on another person or a situation. Often, simply knowing what took place in the child's world in the minutes or hours preceding the action (i.e., the context) can suggest a useful interpretation of the meaning of the particular behavior or behavior pattern being observed. Reading behavior accurately requires an ability to empathize with how young people tend to experience the world and a good understanding of the individual child "being read," and his or her background.

For example, when a child says "I hate you!", an experienced and skilled worker will seek to read this statement as a deeper message. It may indicate that an emotional and painful place has been touched by the worker, and the child is moved from hurt to anger (motive). It may indicate that the youth is seeking a reaction from the worker, perhaps testing the worker's commitment and feelings towards him or her (intent). Or it may simply be the spillover from an unpleasant encounter with someone else, such as a family member calling on the telephone to cancel a planned visit (context). As summed up by an Oriole careworker: "The program boils down to staff being able to understand youth and act appropriately."

As with many other aspects of residential work, only a few of the staff, generally the experienced supervisors or managers, were able to articulate such insights into the nature of their or others' carework practice. This fact demonstrates that mindful or reflective (Schon, 1983) practice is almost impossible for many residential practitioners. For workers to be able to improve their quality of practice, it appears vital that they need to develop an ability to observe and articulate their own actions as well as the actions of those around them. In the current vernacular, it is not enough to "walk the talk," one needs to be able to "talk the walk" as well.

The tendency to use control strategies was seen to correlate with staff who did not involve themselves actively in the lives of the residents. That is, their interactions were not consistently reciprocal, and the daily life of the group care setting lacked a sense of cohesiveness in this regard. This form of staff behavior was frequently referred to as "doing *with*, rather than doing *to*."

Doing With, Not Doing To

All of the group care programs except for Pioneer Place and Parke Street demonstrated significant active involvement by staff *with* the residents whether in meal preparation, house planning, pick-up sports on the driveway, on recreational outings, and the like. The most active involvement of workers in daily activities was observed at Mountainview, where the staff were highly consistent in articulating and applying the principles of experiential education throughout the program. As one worker stated succinctly, "We have to work *with* youth, *not at* them, . . . do *with* the kids, *not to* them. . . ." While the workers felt that they did their best work on wilderness trips where the co-involvement and mutual interdependence was virtually total, they also demonstrated consistent "doing with" at the camp in such activities as cooking, wood cutting, sauna, and dunk in the lake (even through a hole in the ice in winter), and the infamous "morning run" and twenty kilometre finale at the end of the four month stay. This congruence was the product of many years of concerted supervision by the camp manager/supervisor, including weekly staff meetings and two, week-long intensive staff training periods for the entire camp team every year. The struggle for congruence can only be won at a price, and across the well-enough functioning programs, that price was seen to be intensive and ongoing team debriefing and effective supervision. In the words of the manager/supervisor at Mountainview:

> I had to change the whole cultural headset that the staff had and ensure that they were not only listening to kids but were considering what they were saying. I would scrutinize how staff worked with kids, and they had to rationalize what they were doing in a child-centered way. The staff's needs and wants were getting met more than the kids. I took that to heart, and looked to change that in people's headsets.

The staff at Mountainview all echoed this philosophy and approach and respected and admired the manager/supervisor's consistency. A male staff member observed:

> He is very child-centered. He's always working with the child's welfare in mind, not so much with the staff's, though the staff's is important. His priority is delivery to the kid, and he makes that well-known.

A female careworker articulated the approach that the manager/supervisor had created throughout the life and work of the camp as follows: "[Being child-centered], for me, is everything we do here–it's a given. If we have an issue, well, what's best for this person? What's best for that person? Always! It's huge!" The contract manager with the Ministry had high praise for the approach at Mountainview, and indicated how significantly it contrasted with a number of other less effective programs.

SUMMARY

Responding to the resident's pain and pain-based behavior effectively was seen to involve consistent and reciprocal interaction at all levels and at all times, throughout a program's operation, with the flow of congruence beginning with the residence manager and supervisor and cascading down to the daily work of the staff and the daily life of the youth residents. In order to respond consistently and effectively to the residents, staff have to be responding effectively to their own anxiety (pain-based fear), and this process was observed to involve the same ongoing, sensitive, respectful, and expectant responsivity from the supervisor as was required by the residents from the carework staff.

The key psychosocial processes of creating an extrafamilial living environment and responding to pain and pain-based behavior have been seen to define the core challenges for managers, supervisors, and careworkers. However, both of these processes must be defined in relation to serving the best interests of the youth residents, and in order to achieve a significant degree of congruence, they must address the primary goal for the youth themselves, namely developing a sense of normality.

Chapter 7
Developing a Sense of Normality: The Primary Goal for Residents

Our focus, then, becomes one not of our knowing why things happen but of how our clients make sense of their experience and how we might assist them to make sense of things differently.

–Michael Durrant (1993, p. 11)

The residents are the heart of group home life and work. One of the challenges for group home staff is to not allow the necessity of responding to the group to overshadow the need to see and understand each youth as an individual. In the same way that each child will experience his or her family in a different way than their siblings, it is evident that each resident experiences a group home and group home staff members in his or her own unique way. At the same time, the immersion within the daily reality of group home life in this study has revealed a common and primary goal for all residents: *developing a sense of normality.*

It is important to note the nuances in the phrasing of this key psychosocial process. It does not say "developing normality," as this could mislead us into focusing on only the degree to which the young person's behavior complies with some set of expected social or developmental norms. For most of the young people in this study, such compliance was both unrealistic (at least in the short- to mid-term time period) and inappropriate. In order to bring about sustainable psychosocial development for the resident for the longer term, the development of a *sense* of normality (such as a sense of belonging, a sense of self-worth, a sense of trust, or a sense of competence in some activity, and so on) is perhaps attainable, as well as being developmentally appropriate and

[Haworth co-indexing entry note]: "Developing a Sense of Normality: The Primary Goal for Residents." Anglin, James P. Co-published simultaneously in *Child & Youth Services* (The Haworth Press, Inc.) Vol. 24, No. 1/2, 2002, pp. 123-131; and: *Pain, Normality, and the Struggle for Congruence: Reinterpreting Residential Care for Children and Youth* (James P. Anglin) The Haworth Press, Inc., 2002, pp. 123-131. Single or multiple copies of. this article are available for a fee from The Haworth Document Delivery Service [1-800-HAWORTH, 9:00 a.m. - 5:00 p.m. (EST). E-mail address: docdelivery@haworthpress.com].

http://www.haworthpress.com/store/product.asp?sku=J024
10.1300/J024v24n01_08

therapeutic within the transition period offered by a group residential care setting.

To say that a setting offers a resident an opportunity for *developing a sense of normality* is to indicate that the resident has the opportunity to develop an "intuition" of normality or "a capacity to appreciate or understand" some aspect of normality (American Heritage Dictionary, 1970, p. 1180). While a group home is not a "normal" or "natural" living environment for children in general, it is within the ability of a group home setting to offer young people "transitional" and "approximating" experiences that will act as bridges back into full participation in "normal" and "natural" family and community life. It was evident in this research that, for many of the youth placed in group homes, the intimacy and pressures to "be normal" in familial situations was too great for them to handle. As was discussed in relation to the differences between foster homes and group homes in Chapter 5, familial settings cannot generally cope with the sometimes violent and destructive (to self and others, and to property) outbursts and "acting out" that tends to erupt when the pressures become too much for the youth to cope with.

Also, the phrasing of this key psychosocial process does not refer to "being exposed to" a sense of normality, as mere exposure to aspects of normality (while an important part of creating the living environment) is not sufficient in itself to bring about personal learning and self-directed behavior change. In addition to an experience of normality in the environment, there must be a "making of meaning" on the part of the youth in relation to these experiences.

It was evident in this study that the young residents in these group homes had, for the most part, come from deficient living environments and with underdeveloped cognitive abilities relative to their age group. Consequently, they generally lacked the language and concepts with which to make sense of what they saw, heard, and felt. They sometimes needed the guidance of an adult to talk with them about what they were experiencing in order to have that experience "take hold" and become accessible to them within their own cognitive developmental processes and decision-making. On the basis of the interviews and observations with these youth and the staff, it would appear that giving orders, instructions, or advice without modeling through action tends to lead to the development of a sense of mistrust on the part of the residents. Further, in the absence of talking things through (i.e., labeling and exploring the meaning of actions and behaviors), even good modeling will not likely result in the development of the "sense of normality" required for the development of internal controls in youth. As will be explored later in this chapter, the means for facilitating "a sense of normality" needs to be further analyzed in terms of the interactional dynamics that tend to support such a developmental understanding.

Sociologically, the concepts of "normality" and "abnormality" can carry with them many connotations of both an emotional and evaluative kind. The concept of normality can be applied to an environment as well as to an individual's needs or behavior, and in practice the concept of normality involves an interaction between both of these elements. Whether or not a child's behavior is considered within the normal range often depends upon the child's environment and the environment's ability to adapt to the child.

There are at least several senses in which the word "normal" can be used in relation to the process of socialization and human development. "Normal" can simply refer to some form of statistical average that indicates how, in fact, the majority of people, families or organizations function. It can also refer to the range of acceptable behaviors or practices within society and thus represent a broader notion of normality than a statistical average or norm. "Normal" can also be used as a virtual synonym for "healthy" and thus carry with it an implicit or explicit notion of some ideal standard.

Over the course of this study, the concept of normality was evident in a variety of ways and contexts within residential group care life and work. For example:

1. *Home routines,* such as "normal bedtimes." "We have chores, responsibilities and natural and logical consequences, like a family."
2. *Home appearance,* such as, "We put up pictures of the kids and staff . . ."; "The display of the home is important, with the furniture, decorations and so on, right down to the smell of the cleaning liquid we use on the floor."
3. *Child behavior,* such as, "The workers didn't have a real good sense of what was normal. There was no perspective, and some workers over-identified with youth."
4. *Child development,* such as, "We need to teach these kids to be normal, regular 10 year olds."
5. *Family functioning,* such as, "We live together as a family. Most of these kids have not experienced a normal family life."
6. *Socially acceptable behavior,* such as, "We take the kids out to restaurants just so they can learn how to behave in the community as part of a group."

However, no matter how normal or normative group homes try to be, the young people living in them are aware that this is not a "normal" or typical living arrangement for children to grow up in within their communities. It would appear that creating a "sense of normality" for the residents without attempting to pretend that a group home setting is either "normal" or "normative" is vital for their sense of well-being.

A stated goal of a number of the group homes in this study, in tune with the principles of normalization (Wolfensberger, 1972), was to create living environments that have characteristics that are close to the overall community norms. Thus, the physical facilities need to resemble single family dwellings, the program needs to approximate the daily living patterns within the community, and the residents' appearances ought not to set them apart unduly from their peers and neighbors. Indeed, many of the home managers, supervisors, and careworkers in this study emphasized how they were attempting to make the group home feel "as close to a family as possible."

However, it has already been noted in Chapter 5 that, for a variety of possible reasons, what some young people need at certain stages in their development is *not* a family. Rather, what they may need is "a sense of family life." This point is made by Levy (1996) in his discussion of residential education for homeless children:

> An elementary theoretical analysis shows that what a homeless child needs is something that *behaves* and *feels*–to the child–like a family, not simply something that looks like a family from the outside. In today's circumstances, most "warm little homes" that are not natural families–and even many that are–do not and cannot behave like families in this deeper sense. [emphasis in original] (p. 70)

As noted in Chapter 3 when the overall theoretical framework for understanding group home life and work was introduced, a number of interactional dynamics were observed over the course of this study to be important in the creation of a "well-enough" functioning group home environment. In addition, these dynamics were seen to be important at each and every level of the home's operation. It is time to consider how these interactional dynamics impact upon the young residents directly.

THE IMPACT OF KEY INTERACTIONAL DYNAMICS ON THE RESIDENTS

It is perhaps important to reemphasize here that while the group home setting is created for the primary purpose of providing a caring and developmental environment for young people in distress and pain and in this sense is not a naturally occurring arrangement, the relationships and experiences within the setting are, and always will be, fully *real*. At the same time, while the human interactions that take place within the home will always be real experiences involving real persons and relations, there can be a wide range in the developmental or therapeutic value of these interactions. Youth residents and former residents interviewed in this study commented on their different experiences of staff in various settings, and the fact that some staff did not convey much commitment to or even interest in the youth residents. This type of care was derisively labelled by the youth as "babysitting" or "putting in time."

During the field work visits, several workers were seen to approach the carework function as a custodial job, and they did not appear to accord the youth residents much respect and value as persons. As the Pioneer Place supervisor commented, "They don't think these kids are worth it." In this sense, it does happen that some relationships between staff and youth are "phony" and are lacking in warmth, genuineness, and positive regard. The well-enough functioning homes quite consistently demonstrated an awareness of the importance of the interactional dynamics in the home, both those that affected the youth directly and those that affected them indirectly. The supervisor at Dogwood explained:

> Let the kids see you display your relationship building. You have to build a relationship with the co-worker, but you also have to build it with the young person. Kids learn a lot from visuals. They are always watching, and they pick up everything. So, if you can display that relationship with your co-worker in a very safe and appropriate way, the kids will pick up on that, and you set the mood for the house, and that's very important too.

Each of the eleven key interactional dynamics identified initially in Chapter 3 will now be examined in terms of their influence on the residents' primary goal: developing a sense of normality. There are, of course, many aspects of normality, and different experiences and interactions can help the residents to develop various aspects of what could be seen as "an inner compass" by which they can identify, make sense of, and take charge of their own behavior. On the basis of extensive comparative analysis of all of the research data gathered in this study, these eleven dynamics were seen to encompass all of the major interactional processes considered central to the creation of group home life and work by the study participants.

1. *Listening and responding with respect* to youth helps them to develop a sense of dignity, a sense of being valued as persons, and a sense of self-worth.

> The youth are the experts, and we always have to listen to them with real respect. I don't ever want to forget that. (Careworker at Oriole)

2. *Communicating a framework for understanding* with youth helps them to develop a sense of meaning and a sense of the rationality within daily life.

> If you are going to effect change, you have to . . . engage the youth in a dialogue about their needs and wants. We need to engage them and take it

to the next level. It is often said about the kids who come through our program that they are a lot more articulate about their wants and needs than they were before. I mean, kids can really learn to self-advocate through the interaction and the programming. . . . (Manager at Mountain-view)

3. *Building rapport and relationships* with youth helps them to develop a sense of belonging and connectedness with others.

I set out to break my foster homes down as soon as I arrived. I went through thirty foster homes in six years; I was pretty good at it. When I O.D.'d [overdosed] here, the staff sat with me twenty-four hours a day, and I realized that they were not going to let me go. . . . (Former resident of Dogwood)

4. *Establishing structure, routine, and expectations* with youth assists them to develop a sense of order and predictability in the world, as well as a sense of trust in the reliability of others.

Many of these youth never knew where their next meal was coming from or when they were going to be beaten. How can you get on with your life when you live like that? (Careworker at Oriole)

5. *Inspiring commitment* in youth encourages them to develop a sense of value, loyalty, and continuity.

There is such a sense of pride in this place with these guys. It becomes like sacred ground. Many of them return months and years after they leave. . . . Are you still doing the run? And do you jump through the ice? [Those] are the two questions they always ask. (Manager at Mountain-view)

6. *Offering youth emotional and developmental support* helps them to develop a sense of caring and mastery.

I really didn't want to go on the camping trip but they convinced me I could do it. When I stood on the top of that mountain, it was the greatest experience of my life! (Former resident of Mountainview)

7. *Challenging the thinking and actions* of youth helps them to develop a sense of potential and capability.

It's important that the programming challenge the belief system that the kids come to the program with . . . it's all designed so that it's a challenge. It's amazing when they experience success, some for the first time. (Careworker at Mountainview)

8. *Sharing power and decision-making* with youth encourages them to develop a sense of personal power and discernment.

> I guess it all comes down to the relationships that you hope to build with kids; to be able to dialogue about making good decisions. . . . "You've lost your personal power, don't you want to get it back?" They are marginalized to the point where they don't have a choice. They need social skills and the ability to advocate. They need to prove to themselves that they can make good decisions and then advocate for themselves. (Careworker at Mountainview)

9. *Respecting the personal space and time* of young people helps them to develop a sense of independence.

> They need to be able to make mistakes, and at their own pace, and know that they will still be respected. (Careworker at Mountainview)

10. *Discovering and uncovering the potential* of youth helps them to develop a sense of hope and opportunity.

> I will advocate for kids. I'll go tooth and claw to defend our philosophy. "[These kids] are *not* animals, and they are *full* of potential, and you have no idea what they are capable of. So, don't you dare judge them, you bonehead, narrow-minded right wing person!" (Careworker at Mountainview)

11. *Providing resources* to youth helps them to develop a sense of gratitude and generosity.

> When I left the home, [the manager] gave me a brand new fly-fishing rod. Wow! I couldn't believe it! (Former resident at Yellowdale)

The process of responding in a healthy manner to the youth is often referred to in the group homes as "modeling," a process that represents an important means of achieving congruence in service of the children's best interests. The supervisor at Mountainview summed it up: "I wanted [staff] doing positive adult modeling. That is another cornerstone of the whole process, mirroring what we expect students to do."

Also in the Mountainview program, a worker talked about "caring to confront." This worker had experienced an adolescence similar to that of many of the youth in the camp, characterized by rebellion against authority, abuse of drugs and alcohol, and some criminal activity. As a result, he was not easily manipulated or conned by the behavior of the young men, and he frequently confronted them with his observations and his interpretations of their behavior. However, he did it from a place of empathy and caring, and the residents noted this in their discussions about how they experienced the care they were receiving from him. Youth discern very quickly whether staff members are genuinely committed to them and their developmental needs or whether they are "putting in time" and "are in it for the buck."

The feedback from youth who have been in care demonstrates how vital it is that all careworkers understand the moral and ethical dimensions to their practice, and see their work not as "just a job" but as an influential and demanding practice with important and potentially life-long implications for the experiences and development of the youth in care. More important than the structure or setting of the group home in conveying a sense of normality to youth is the experiencing of the staff as persons by the youth. "I am a basketball player, and [George] is a mountain climber. The kids need to see that I am not just a child care worker" (Careworker at Oriole).

What does it take to create a sense of normality for young people in a group home setting? As noted in Chapter 4, the data from this study suggest that there needs to be a high level of congruence across all levels of the group home's functioning. First and foremost, there needs to be an explicit understanding on the part of the staff at all levels about the fundamental values and beliefs characteristic of the home. This may involve the drafting of a mission statement (as at Mountainview) or a program philosophy statement (as at Yellowdale) but, as previously indicated, most staff will take their primary cues from the verbal communications from the manager and supervisor.

Also seen to be important is the ongoing dialogue amongst the staff members at all levels concerning what the home stands for, is trying to achieve, and considers to be good practice and in the children's best interests. The well-enough functioning settings in this study accomplished this process in staff meetings and in interchanges between staff members while on shift and at shift changes. The staff members in poorly functioning programs exhibited little dialogue related to any of the core processes of group home life and work, talked mainly about relatively inconsequential matters in staff shift changes and meetings, and exhibited confusion as to both individual child and program goals.

SUMMARY

There are many facets of normality that are addressed, effectively or ineffectively, within the living environment of a group home setting. These include home routines, home appearance, child behavior, child development, family functioning, and socially acceptable personal presentation. However, beyond the creation of a normative set of expectations and activities is the development of a *sense* of normality on the part of the residents. While a group home is not a "normal" or "natural" setting for young people in our communities, residents are able to develop a sense of normality across numerous dimensions of their development even within such an "artificial" environment.

For many young people, prior to being ready to live in a family situation, they need to experience a sense of family life and family-like relationships characterized by a sense of belonging, caring, respect, loyalty, trust, generosity and so on. On the basis of the data gathered in this research, it would appear that one of the strengths of staffed group homes is that they are well-suited to providing a sense of intimacy without much of the usual emotional baggage associated with living in a family.

Chapter 8

Through the Lens
of the Theoretical Framework:
A Review of Selected Residential Child
and Youth Care Literature

Some scientists (the researchers) concentrate their time providing the facts; others (the theorists) build alternative frameworks into which the facts may be fitted.

–Neil Agnew and Sandra Pyke (1982, p. 11)

It is the theory that determines what we can observe.

–Albert Einstein, as remarked to Heisenberg (Reay, 1986, p. 51)

The purpose of this chapter is twofold: (a) to provide a brief overview of relevant residential care literature, and (b) to examine some key texts in order to determine how the proposed framework reinforces, adds to, overlooks, or contradicts the findings and formulations of related studies.

OVERVIEW OF RELEVANT LITERATURE

A review of existing literature on residential care reveals that there are very few Canadian studies of any description, a somewhat larger number originating within the United States and Israel, and a considerable body of research undertaken in the United Kingdom. While a systematic review of the broader

[Haworth co-indexing entry note]: "Through the Lens of the Theoretical Framework: A Review of Selected Residential Child and Youth Care Literature." Anglin, James P. Co-published simultaneously in *Child & Youth Services* (The Haworth Press, Inc.) Vol. 24, No. 1/2, 2002, pp. 133-151; and: *Pain, Normality, and the Struggle for Congruence: Reinterpreting Residential Care for Children and Youth* (James P. Anglin) The Haworth Press, Inc., 2002, pp. 133-151. Single or multiple copies of this article are available for a fee from The Haworth Document Delivery Service [1-800-HAWORTH, 9:00 a.m. - 5:00 p.m. (EST). E-mail address: docdelivery@haworthpress.com].

http://www.haworthpress.com/store/product.asp?sku=J024
10.1300/J024v24n01_09

European literature was not undertaken as part of this study due to difficulties of access and translation, a useful overview of the state of residential care in eighteen European countries can be found in Gottesman (1991).

The Independent Review into Residential Care undertaken by Gillian Wagner (Wagner, 1988) appeared to signal a reawakening of a strong government interest in residential care within the United Kingdom, and it provided a launching point for a major program of research over the subsequent decade. A series of twelve studies commissioned by the Department of Health, most of which were published in 1998, offers perhaps the most comprehensive single body of research into the various facets of residential care ever undertaken on a systematic and coterminous basis (Department of Health, 1998). Also, Bullock, Little, and Millham (1993) offer a comprehensive overview of over one hundred residential research studies undertaken prior to 1993, for the most part published in the United Kingdom, but with some references drawn from the United States, Israel, and Europe.

In Canada, only two published texts presenting empirical research studies on residential care were identified (Palmer, 1976; Reichertz, 1978). The Reichertz study will be examined in more detail in the following section. Most of the remaining literature consists of occasional journal articles, book chapters, policy and standards documents, and collections of perspectives presented at conferences. For example, a major report of the Commission on Emotional and Learning Disorders in Children, published as "One million children–the CELDIC report" (1970), generated a background report "Children in Canada: Residential Care" (Rae-Grant & Moffat, 1971). This study was, overall, quite scathing in its assessment of residential care and treatment. Such phrases as "cannibalistic of scarce professional staff," "prodigal rather than parsimonious of resources," "a drastic interruption of the normal pattern," and "always compounds difficulties or creates them" (Rae-Grant & Moffat, 1971, p. 100) illustrate its orientation.

In 1975, an inventory of residential services for children in Canada was published by the Canadian Council on Social Development (Hepworth, 1975), followed in 1977 by a collection of articles on various aspects of services, including residential care and treatment, published in celebration of the twentieth anniversary of Thistletown Regional Centre in Ontario (Shamsie, 1977). The perspectives in the latter volume were mainly focused on programs operated in Ontario and were written by Ontario-based practitioners largely drawing upon their own clinical experiences.

A little over a decade later, the first comprehensive text on professional child and youth care was edited by faculty members from the School of Child and Youth Care at the University of Victoria (Denholm, Ferguson, & Pence, 1993). This text included a brief overview of residential child care in Canada, and the chapter concluded that "residential programs should continue to be viewed as an integral part of the continuum of services to troubled youngsters and their families" (Fewster & Garfat, 1987).

In 1991, an article on residential care in Canada was included in an international text on residential care providing a brief historical review, an overview of national programs, policies, treatment models, staffing, training, management approaches, and societal attitudes (Anglin, 1991). In the same year, a clinically-oriented text was published that included a brief analysis of residential treatment from a psychiatric perspective, and it concluded that such placements were only helpful for defusing crisis situations and for providing a brief "cooling-off" period for the shortest possible time (Steinhauer, 1991, p. 280). In brief, prior to this group home research project, only two major research studies on residential care have been published in Canada, along with a number of surveys, program overviews, and practice-oriented perspectives.

In the United States, the first text on residential care and treatment was published in 1935 (Aichhorn, 1935) and was written originally in German in 1925 based upon clinical experiences of the author in Austria. A variety of books followed, with some of the most notable authors being Bettleheim (1950, 1955, 1967, 1974), Redl and Wineman (1951, 1952), Polsky (1962), Polsky and Claster, (1968), Treischman, Whittaker, and Brendtro (1969), Whittaker and Treischman (1972), Whittaker (1979), Hobbs (1982), Brendtro and Ness (1983), Beker and Eisikovits (1991), and Beker and Magnuson (1996). Most of these texts were based on the extensive practice experience of the authors or other invited contributors. Polsky's participant observation study in a children's cottage is a notable exception.

Israeli authors have also been quite prolific with a variety of practice and research texts being published on residential education and care (e.g., Arieli, Kashti & Shlasky, 1983; Eisikovits & Beker, 1986; Gottesmann, 1991, 1994; Levy, 1993; Wolins & Gottesmann, 1971; Wozner, 1991). The Wozner (1991) text is particularly interesting in the context of this study, as it is the only other attempt to develop a comprehensive schema for residential care (albeit for all "people care" institutions). Therefore, it will be analyzed in some depth in the detailed text review section of this chapter. One additional book on residential treatment by an Australian therapist (Durrant, 1993) will also be reviewed in the text analysis section, as it is a relatively recent publication that echoes a number of the key themes uncovered in the group home study.

ANALYSIS OF SELECTED TEXTS

As the intention is to be illustrative rather than comprehensive in examining the framework resulting from this study, ten books on residential group care have been chosen to provide a selective analysis in order to "test" the framework for its fit, relevance, and utility in light of the existing residential care literature.

In relation to assessing a theory or theoretical framework, Glaser makes the following comment on the nature of grounded theories in particular: "Grounded theories have 'grab' and they are interesting. People remember them; they use them. To achieve this use . . . a theory must have fit and relevance, and it must work" (Glaser, 1978, p. 4).

Since the research and publication flow in the United Kingdom has been quite plentiful, all of the books selected from the U.K. for purposes of this illustrative review are recent, with only one before 1998. On the other hand, given the dearth of residential child and youth care research studies published in North America, this selection includes books published in 1935, 1969, 1978, 1991, and 1993. This look "through the lens of the theoretical framework" will begin with a review of the five studies undertaken in the United Kingdom, commencing with two studies initiated by David Berridge (Berridge, 1985; Berridge & Brodie, 1998).

The United Kingdom

Children's Homes (Berridge, 1985), and Children's Homes Revisited (Berridge & Brodie, 1998). The initial study by Berridge (1998) drew its sample of 20 homes from a set of residences roughly comparable to eight of the homes in this study. (The wilderness correctional camp and the staff-supported foster home included for comparative purposes in this study lie outside of the Berridge sample.) However, there is sufficient similarity overall to make for a useful comparison of both the research method and the study findings.

Berridge (1985) states in the introduction to his first book that the objective of his study "is to provide new empirical information on an important area of social policy by looking at a group of institutions which have previously received scant attention" (p. 10). While the present study shares Berridge's desire to address an understudied phenomenon, namely, group care residences, the aim of the present study was quite different, that is, to develop a theoretical framework in order to better understand the functioning of such residences. Thus, the Berridge (1985) study was designed to be primarily descriptive in nature whereas the current study was primarily theoretical in intent.

Another significant difference between the studies relates to the research design and instrumentation. Whereas Berridge began with a conceptual framework by which the homes would be "systematically explored" (1985, p. 11), with a set of interview guides and measuring instruments, the current study began with a general list of questions and a set of research procedures necessary for undertaking a grounded theory study.

As a result of the different aims and methods, the outcomes of the two studies differ quite significantly. While the Berridge (1985) study provides very detailed information on the residents, staff and homes, the current study offers only broad profiles. The Berridge text also offers three brief case studies of young people living in the homes. Some of the major findings of the Berridge (1985) study include:

1. Few staff had experienced relevant professional training (p. 65).
2. There is a clear imbalance between the needs of children and existing staff structures in terms of staff training, involvement of men and women, recruitment of ethnic minorities, and changing conditions of work (p. 65).
3. There is an incongruity between children's needs and residential styles of the homes (p. 85).
4. The quality of individual care offered was, generally, of acceptable standard, and in several establishments was extremely impressive (p. 86).
5. A significant proportion of children referred to children's homes has experienced "fostering failure" and these residents can make considerable demands on residential staff (p. 110).
6. Most children maintained family links, and many of these adolescents rejected fostering because of their family situation (p. 110).
7. The problem of leaving care requires further attention (p. 111).
8. Children in residential care usually achieved poorly in school (p. 120).
9. There is a lack of continuity of services between fostering and residential care (p. 120).
10. "The most important findings to emerge from this study include lack of specialisation in the children's homes and the incongruence between residential styles and the children's needs and problems" (Berridge, 1985, p. 127).

Interestingly, all of these findings were also findings of this study. Especially intriguing is the fact that the concept of "incongruence" is shared as an element of the major findings of both studies. However, the notion of incongruence is addressed in somewhat different ways within the two studies with the current study exploring this aspect in somewhat more depth within and across the levels of operation of the homes as well as in relation to the three identified core psychosocial processes. Reviewing the three case studies of "Donna," "Trevor," and "Pauline" in Berridge (1985, pp. 43-53), it is striking how the descriptions of the background experiences and demonstrated behaviors echo the notion of "pain and pain-based behavior" discovered in the current study. Further, while the three case studies do not explore the concept of pain explicitly, the acknowledgement section at the beginning of the book states, "I am particularly grateful . . . to the children for re-living and recounting some of the pain which they and their families had endured and which we can hardly begin to understand" (Berridge, 1985, p. vii). Clearly, the experience of pain and its effects on the children made a powerful impression on the researchers in both studies, but the significance of this pain is given different emphasis in each one.

Creating an extrafamilial living environment is explored by Berridge (1985, pp. 70-73), particularly on the familial and extrafamilial dimension, while developing a sense of normality is not addressed to any significant degree. In conclusion, it would appear that the two studies are very complementary, with the Berridge study presenting significantly more detailed profiles on various aspects of the homes and a primary focus on policy and practice issues and questions. The current study, on the other hand, offers a more explicit framework within which some of the important issues raised by Berridge could perhaps be more fully explored and understood in relation to one another.

In the mid-1990s, Berridge was joined by Brodie (Berridge & Brodie, 1998) in an update of the 1985 study. The original intention of *Children's Homes Revisited* was to revisit the same sample of homes across the three counties ten years later. However, only four of the homes were still open with two of these due for imminent closure (p. 28). The 1995 sample contained twelve homes, with two of them serving children with severe learning disabilities and additional health needs (p. 30). While the study was still being undertaken within a primarily policy-related paradigm, a major addition to the research design was a component enabling the researchers to analyze, in greater detail than the first study, the quality of care offered within the homes (p. 9). Some of the major findings of the 1998 study will be outlined below. Many of them are articulated in terms of the changes noted since the 1985 study.

1. The number of young people in a residence had dropped significantly since 1985, and the staff-to-child ratios had improved (p. 160).
2. The number of residents posing behavioral problems prior to entry had more than doubled (p. 161).
3. While levels of qualification among staff had improved, about 80 percent of staff remained unqualified (p. 161).
4. Problems of behavioral control had significantly increased, and staff lacked confidence in how to deal with young people's indiscipline (p. 161).
5. Homes received less external management attention and did not comply with some basic legislative requirements in terms of basic documentation (p. 161).
6. There were exacerbated problems in liasion with fieldwork colleagues (p. 162).
7. Relationships with parents were noticeably stronger (p. 162).

8. The quality of care was seen to be very uneven across the sample (p. 162).
9. "The strongest relationship we uncovered with the quality of care provided by the home was the extent to which the head of home could specify a clear theoretical or therapeutic orientation, or at least methods of work for the home" (p. 163).

Once again, as with the 1985 study, the major finding of the 1998 study closely echoed an important aspect of the major theme of the framework developed from the current research. Specifically, point 9 above parallels the flow of congruence discovered within the homes involved in the current study. Further, in their discussion, Berridge and Brodie (1998, p. 163) use such concepts as "coherence," "consistency," and "discontinuity," again echoing the notion of the struggle for congruence. Also, they note that "there was more confusion about objectives and working methods concerning adolescents" (p. 173), suggesting the need for a clear, accessible and useful framework that could offer a degree of understanding and some guidance for practice.

An additional important linkage between the 1998 Berridge and Brodie study and the present study is noted in relation to the psychosocial process of responding to pain and pain-based behavior. Berridge and Brodie observe that "staff attitudes and responsiveness have a major influence on children's residential experiences" (p. 144), and this comment is embedded within a discussion of "control problems," children's feelings of "anxiety and insecurity," and the experience of "behavioral problems." Thus overall, there appears to be a significant degree of congruence between the findings of both of Berridge's studies and the elements identified in this study's theoretical framework. The major differences in the findings reflect different intentions (i.e., descriptive–Berridge, 1985; descriptive/evaluative–Berridge & Brodie, 1998; and theoretical–Anglin, current document) as well as corresponding differences in method.

The next two texts from the United Kingdom have been selected from a dozen important and linked studies commissioned by the Department of Health to address key concerns arising from public inquiries (Department of Health, 1998). These two exemplars offer some comparability in breadth of interest and scope of concern in relation to the present study. Space does not allow for an analysis of all twelve studies here. However, summaries and conclusions of all of the projects are provided in the useful compendium, *Caring for Children Away from Home: Messages from Research* (Department of Health, 1998). While it was not one of the originally commissioned studies, the Berridge and Brodie (1998) text is also included in the compendium.

Making Residential Care Work: Structure and Culture in Children's Homes (Brown, Bullock, Hobson, & Little, 1998). Early in their introduction,

Brown et al. (1998) state that "(W)hat is agreed by most professionals is that to get a high quality service, the different aspects of residential care have to be complementary. Terms such as 'concordance,' 'balance' and 'congruence' would form the building blocks of any discourse on residential care" (p. 2).

This common wisdom of professionals involved in residential care was well and truly confirmed by the framework that emerged from this grounded theory study, as the notion of congruence was found to be central to the functioning of all of the group care settings in this study. The Brown et al. (1998) study examined "nine unremarkable establishments" (p. 5) over a period of a year, whereas this study examined ten homes over fourteen months, but with "on-site" time frames varying from several weeks to about ten months. However, the present study inquired into resident, staff, home, and agency changes over a twelve month period in an attempt to take into account the developmental changes characteristic of an annual cycle in the life of homes.

A major conclusion of the Brown (1998) et al. study is the following:

> The relationship between a home's structure and culture has already been established; a good structure leads to a concordant staff culture, which in turn leads to a concordant child culture. This chapter and its predecessor, looking at outcomes for homes and the individuals in them, add the final components to the study. They demonstrate that concordance between a home's structure and between the structure and culture (staff and child) results in a good home, and a good home leads to better outcomes for children. (p. 116)

The concept of the flow of congruence key to the present study is also reflected in the Brown et al. (1998) study as it was in Berridge and Brodie (1998). However, the different research methods used in the different studies mean that, while their conceptualizations are very complementary, each study offers a somewhat different picture of the structure, functioning, and outcomes of a group care setting. The Brown et al. (1998) text presents a useful analysis of homes in relation to the *Looking After Children* outcome framework (Parker, Ward, Jackson, Aldgate, & Wedge, 1991; Ward, 1995) and the principles of the Children Act introduced in England in 1989.

Children's Homes: A Study in Diversity (Sinclair & Gibbs, 1998). The central aim of the Sinclair and Gibbs study was "to measure and explain the different outcomes achieved in the homes," and the study included a large sample of 48 children's homes in the United Kingdom utilizing a comparative and longitudinal research design (1998, pp. 1-8). Like the Berridge studies, this was a descriptive research project gathering "detailed qualitative information" as a basis on which "to measure and explain the different outcomes achieved by the homes" (p. 1).

In light of the present study's framework, and the discovery of the centrality and importance of the process of responding to pain and pain-based behavior, it was striking that in the Sinclair and Gibbs (1998) book, while the notion of the psychoemotional pain of the residents is lightly touched on in only two places in the core of the text (pp. 124 and 190), the following statement was made toward the end of the introductory acknowledgements: "Children's homes are complex exercises in the management of human pain" (p. xvi). There is a suggestion in the chapter on Residents' Behaviour and Subjective Well-Being (p. 190) that staff "would often prefer not to know how miserable [the residents] were." If indeed a central concern of group homes for youth is "the management of human pain" (as both Sinclair and Gibbs' study and the present study would strongly suggest), then it would seem critically important to open up this difficult area for extensive examination, as disturbing as the process might be for all concerned. It would appear that most current research studies are not penetrating this layer of seeming denial and defensiveness, and it was the experience of the current study that it took many months of intensive involvement for both the careworkers and the researcher to be ready to face it and explore it.

In relation to congruence and the flow of congruence, the Sinclair and Gibbs (1998) study identifies evidence for this theme from a number of previous studies. "Links were found between variables connected with the organisation of the establishment (e.g., the autonomy given to staff), the characteristics and attitudes of the staff and the reactions of the residents" (Sinclair and Gibbs, 1998, p. 7).

Sinclair and Gibbs (1998) confirm that "the relationships between the head and the external management are very important" (p. 215). However, they do not emphasize on the basis of their own work the full "flow of congruence" from this top level of interaction right down to the youth residents that is described here. Overall, it would appear that the present study offers an overarching theme along with a coherent set of psychosocial processes, interactional dynamics, and levels of home operation that that would assist in placing many of the facts and issues documented in the Sinclair and Gibbs (1998) study within an encompassing theoretical framework that could add further explanatory power to their findings.

Understanding Residential Child Care (Frost, Mills, & Stein, 1999). This work by Frost, Mills, and Stein seeks to provide "a framework for direct practice" (1999, p. 2) and thus can offer a comparative perspective on this aim that is shared with the present study. However, the development of the Frost, Mills, and Stein framework is not based in an empirical research process but rather has sought to draw from an analysis of a range of existing "historical, theoretical, policy, managerial, and practice perspectives" (p. 2). As such their framework is deduced from other theoretical frameworks (p. 4) rather than induced from social data in the manner of the present grounded theory study. In their introductory chapter, the authors make clear their foundational premise right from the start: "We are committed to the concept of empowerment as a model for child welfare practice" (Frost, Mills, & Stein, 1999, p. 2). Empowerment is seen as the "key connecting idea" (p. 3) or central theme around which the rest of residential care work can be examined and understood. ·

The authors describe their process as follows: "The aims of the chapter are to examine a range of prominent theoretical frameworks, and to develop a contemporary theoretical framework which will inform the empowering practice which we wish to promote" (Frost, Mills & Stein, 1999, p. 27). Further, they say that "we conceptualize [empowerment] as a more complex idea than 'promoting the best interests of the child'" (p. 3). It is far from clear that the idea of empowerment is necessarily more complex than "best interests" and, in fact, empowerment could be understood as but one of the ways (and perhaps, as Frost, Mills and Stein maintain, even the best way) of achieving children's best interests. Therefore, the two concepts can be understood as complementary rather than as mutually exclusive. For example, one could affirm and espouse the critical importance of empowerment of young people and still ask, "And what else is important to ensure children's best interests? Children, especially in their early years, require more than an opportunity to become empowered, surely?"

A number of the emphases in the Frost, Mills, and Stein (1999) text are echoed in the present study, including the significance of consistency and supervision. "Particularly important in working with young people is consistency. . . . A well-organized and well-resourced supervisory program can play an important role in supporting staff in the task of empowering children and young people" (p. 102).

At the same time, a major difference between the Frost, Mills, and Stein approach and the present study is the sociopolitical emphasis of the former as compared to the psychosocial focus of the latter, not unsurprisingly reflecting the significant differences in their methods (i.e., theoretical-deductive versus empirical-inductive). Given that both works seek to offer a relevant and useful framework for practice, the relative merits of the two approaches could best be assessed by practitioners who read and attempt to apply them in their residential work. It is to be hoped that both of these texts will indeed be read, and that they will both be seen to have some utility for their intended purposes.

In differing ways, and to varying degrees, all of the studies originating in the United Kingdom echo the present study's discovery of the importance of the notion of congruence. Some even emphasize the dynamic referred to in this study as the flow of congruence. Also, many of the practice processes and dynamics are similarly echoed through most of the studies, including such aspects as coherent management, the key role of supervision, and the creation of a unique, extrafamilial living environment.

Perhaps the major element in the present study that is only briefly alluded to in the U.K. studies is pain and pain-based behavior (Berridge, 1985, p. 7; Clough, 2000, p. 61; Sinclair & Gibbs, 1998, p. xvi). This lack of emphasis in the U.K. studies appears to have led to an underemphasis on several other key elements in the present framework: the ways of responding (rather then reacting) to such behavior, the critical need to address the pain and pain-based behavior of staff members, and the significance of the process of developing a sense of normality on the part of the young residents in order for changes engendered within the homes to have a degree of transfer beyond young people's residence in the homes. It is, of course, possible that the characteristics of the populations sampled in the present study and in the United Kingdom studies could account for this difference in emphasis. However, there is at least a suggestion in several of the texts reviewed that this pain may be quite comparable across all of the studies.

Finally, of the U.K. studies, only the Frost, Mills, and Stein (1999) text attempted to formulate an explicit theory or theoretical framework for practice. The divergent, though perhaps complementary, formulations that emerged in the two studies reflect the different methods utilized.

Texts Published in North America

Wayward Youth (Aichhorn, 1935). The name "August Aichhorn" has been whispered on the wind in child and youth care for many years. Many of the major North American texts pay homage to this pioneer who moved from Austria to the United States before the Second World War (see, for example, Bettelheim, 1950; Brendtro & Ness, 1983; Redl & Wineman, 1952; Trieschman, Whittaker, & Brendtro, 1969; Whittaker, 1979), but his book has long been out of print and he is almost never read by contemporary workers. With a Foreword written by Sigmund Freud, it should be no surprise to learn that Dr. Aichhorn's orientation was psychoanalytic, and that his text focused on "the application of psychoanalysis to the treatment of delinquent youth" (Aichhorn, 1935, p. 3). The term "wayward," Aichhorn explains, also refers to "so-called problem children and others suffering from neurotic symptoms" (1935, p. 3).

In the latter portion of his book, Aichhorn turns his attention to young people in training schools.

The problem of grouping is not solved merely by bringing children together in the expectation that the interaction of their psychic mechanisms will operate therapeutically. Conditions other than those of the personality of the individual pupils must be considered. I refer to those external conditions which in general constitute the milieu. Not only are the companions with whom one lives important to the dissocial child, but also the material world around him; not only the *milieu* of the group but also the institution as a whole. (Aichhorn, 1935, p. 146; emphasis in original)

Thus, there is an appreciation of the wholeness of institutional life in the care and treatment of young people evident in Aichhorn's writings. He sees, as it were, the psyche-in-context.

Specific educational methods are far less important than an attitude which brings the child into contact with reality. We must give the pupils experiences which fit them for life outside and not for the artificial life of an institution. The more the life of the institution conforms to an actual social community, the more certain is the social rehabilitation of the child. There is a great danger in an institution that the individuality of the child does not develop along lines best suited to his needs but that rules are laid down in accordance with administrative requirements which reduce the child to a mere inmate with a number. (Aichhorn, 1935, p. 150)

He understood from his clinical experience that the whole organization needed to be crafted in service of the child's interests and not for administrative convenience or in service of some fad or ideology. "This method seems to contradict the present popular belief that the best education means letting the child do as he likes. . . . We consider that these continual limitations of his freedom are in the child's interest . . ." (Aichhorn, 1935, p. 194).

Further, to a degree the flow of congruence was also recognized, even if couched in the somewhat sexist conceptions characteristic of the times.

It was especially noticeable in those groups directed by women that a bad mood in the leader would communicate itself to the children, who in turn reacted unfavourably, until the situation became intensified to the point of open conflict. At that time I had no understanding of the cathartic effect of talking things over, but I did notice how the mood of the whole group changed with the mood of the teacher. . . . The attitude of the worker toward the leader determines of itself the relationship between the worker and the child. (Aichhorn, 1935, pp. 153-154)

Even the themes of pain and pain-based behavior and of developing a sense of normality are intimated in Aichhorn's analysis of the residential experience and its antecedents.

Re-education, however, is not achieved through words, admonition, scolding, or punishment, but through what the child actually experiences. Through the milieu we created in our institution and through our type of leadership, we had opportunities every day to give the children experiences the deep effect of which helped to relieve their dissocial behaviour. Often we made use of the mood of the moment or created a situation to produce the desired mood. . . . However varied their behaviour was, it always gave us some hint of what was going on inside our charges. . . . I always found that [a child's] hate is a reaction to an unsatisfied need for love. . . . The small child is subjected repeatedly to disappointments. The expected satisfaction is not achieved and pain instead of pleasure is experienced. . . . Naturally this adjustment is not achieved all at once. It is rather the result of a long process of development. From the unconscious, the ego receives information about physical functions, and through the sense organs about events in the outer world. Thus gradually it becomes capable of conforming to the demands of life. (Aichhorn, 1935, pp. 163-164, p. 189)

It is intriguing to find echoes of the findings of the present research study in an analysis formulated over seventy-five years previous. It leads one to believe that at least some of the core elements of residential life and work have a degree of universality to them that needs to be continually revisited as social and cultural contexts change.

The next text selected, *The Other 23 Hours,* is considered a "classic" in the residential child and youth care literature in North America.

The Other 23 Hours: Child-Care Work with Emotionally Disturbed Children in a Therapeutic Milieu (Trieschman, Whittaker, & Brendtro, 1969). In the Preface, the authors state:

It was our aim in writing *The Other 23 Hours* to bridge somewhat the gap that exists between the theoretical expertise of the professional clinician on the one hand and the very practical, often mundane problems of those who live with the children for the 23 hours apart from the therapy hour. . . . Essentially, the book attempts to do two things: to shed some light on the major routines of the day . . . and to deal at length with two phenomena that are part and parcel of every children's institution: the temper tantrum and the therapeutic relationship. (Trieschman, Whittaker, & Brendtro, 1969, p. xii)

The scope and aims of *The Other 23 Hours* can be seen to be somewhat more narrow than those of the much more recent studies undertaken in the United Kingdom. The writing was based on the authors' considerable clinical

experience, mainly obtained at the Walker Home for Children in Massachusetts and their previous academic training.

> The theoretical underpinnings of this book derive essentially from three
> different areas: psychoanalytic ego psychology, the "life space" model
> of Redl, and some of the new sociobehavioural theories. If *The Other 23
> Hours* is able to make a substantive and practical contribution to the
> statement that "the child-care worker is the most important figure in the
> institution," then our major purpose will have been well served.
> (Trieschman, Whittaker, & Brendtro, 1969, p. xiii)

This eclectic introduction to many of the challenging aspects of front-line
residential work represented a breakthrough when published and to this day
offers an important validation of much of what many careworkers have known
or known about without being able to articulate it so thoroughly and learnedly.
The present study has attempted to create a conceptual framework that would
similarly validate the knowledge and practice of careworkers and allied staff
members and also move beyond practice wisdom into proposing the core elements of a theory to help guide and support group home practice.

The third North American text selected is, to the my knowledge, the only
Canadian book published on an empirical research study of residential care for
young people prior to the current study, and the two are separated in time by almost a quarter of a century. If for no other reason, both studies should be worthy of note.

*Residential Care: The Impact of Institutional Policies, Structures, and Staff
on Residential Children (Reichertz, 1978).* In the words of Reichertz, "this research project was designed to evaluate the impact on children in institutional
programs for dependent, neglected, delinquent, and emotionally disturbed children" (1978, p. xiv). The project involved the study of nine English-speaking
institutions for children and youth in Montreal over a two-year period. Some of
the organizations involved in the study encompassed a variety of residential
settings. One, for example, consisted of ten group homes totaling seventy
young residents. The study was stimulated by the Model of Community-Ori-
ented Care developed by Dr. George Thomas in the United States (Thomas,
1975), and the instruments developed by Thomas were utilized to evaluate the
institutions selected in the Montreal study (Reichertz, 1978, p. xiv). Reichertz'
overall findings on the effects of institutional living on the children are worthy
of mention.

> In general, the data indicated that children in residential care continued to
> develop normally. In fact, children often made substantial improvement.
> Thus the findings from this study should minimise the worries expressed

by critics of residential care. These institutional environments were less powerful and less destructive than many would have thought. (Reichertz, 1978, p. 302)

In relation to congruence, Reichertz made the following observations.

The institutional environment has an effect on the staff members as well as resident children. The power of the institutional process of socialization was evidenced by the fact that the attitudes of staff members had a remarkable tendency to converge. If the attitudes of an employee did not coincide with the attitudes of his peers, the employee tended to modify his attitudes or to leave his job. Because both clients and employees need to have a strong belief in an optimistic and explanatory treatment philosophy, administrators must maintain high staff morale in the face of exhausting and frustrating work. Staff need structures [sic] opportunities for training and supervision, and, in general, the effects of peer socialization must be carefully attended. (Reichertz, 1978, p. 316)

In terms of the advantages offered by group homes over larger institutional environments, Reichertz says that "the advantage derives from the fact that with the creation of living conditions which offer the maximum degree of normalcy and which produce growth in the group home setting, a broad range of children can potentially benefit" (Reichertz, 1978, p. 324).

The methods of a highly structured approach and the focus on applying existing tools to the measurement of a wide range of predetermined variables could hardly have been more different from the approach of the present study. While there are echoes of similar findings across several dimensions, the present study's initial open engagement without the use of preconceived frameworks and its aim to discover and articulate a grounded theoretical framework make any further comparison difficult and not very fruitful.

Moving away from North America, one Australian and one Israeli book that are particularly relevant in the context of the findings of the current study will round out the analysis of selected texts.

Other Texts

Residential Treatment: A Cooperative, Competency-Based Approach to Therapy and Program Design (Durrant, 1993). Durrant offers a therapeutic framework primarily grounded in his own extensive practice experience in residential programs. He offers "some ways of thinking about the process of residential treatment" (p. x) that draw heavily upon brief interactional and family systems approaches to therapy. In introducing his book, he emphasizes that "without some theory, we lack any consistency in our work" (p. xiii). Echoing the idea of developing a sense of normality, Durrant states that "therapy should be about establishing conditions in which people can make sense of themselves differently" (p. 10). He also emphasizes that "the entire context of the residential program . . . may be seen as 'the therapy'" (Durrant, p. 159), echoing the core process of creating an extrafamilial living environment. Further, Durrant also touches on the third core psychosocial process of responding to pain and pain-based behavior towards the end of his book in a brief section on "meaning vs. emotion" (pp. 186-188).

> Nothing in the range of the brief or family therapies changes what we already know about people needing to feel validated, to experience empathic responses from the professionals with who they have contact. Anything less becomes the application of technique without any real respect or genuineness. The question becomes one not of "*Do* we take feelings into account?" but rather "*How* do we take them into account?" My belief is that acknowledgement of feelings is crucial but is not in itself what brings about change. (p. 187)

Durrant goes on to discuss his belief that while emotions (such as pain) need to be acknowledged, they are not paramount. The emotions need to be acknowledged in order that people will feel heard and respected, and the main emphasis is on developing "new views of self" (p. 188). Thus, Durrant's therapeutic framework seems very compatible with the theoretical framework emerging from this study, and each echoes elements of the other. The major differences relate to the fact that the group home framework was derived from using the grounded theory method, and the Durrant framework was derived from clinical practice and therapeutic perspectives, hence the former's more conceptual nature and the latter's pronounced clinical or practice flavor.

The last text to be reviewed in this section appears to be the only other study of residential care that attempts to construct a conceptual framework, or "schema," the word used by the author.

People Care in Institutions: A Conceptual Schema and Its Application (Wozner, 1991). It is perhaps important to note that Wozner's framework has been developed for application to all forms of residential institutions and not only for young people but also for adults, encompassing such diverse settings as foundling homes, monasteries, prisons, health resorts, and military training camps. To denote this broad spectrum of residential settings, Wozner has coined the term "internats." Therefore, his scope is clearly much broader than that of the group home study. Nevertheless, Wozner's conceptions frequently echo the findings of this study.

Internats are artificial but often used environments in which people live some part of their lives. The quality of an internat is the product of the intentions of the people who organize it. . . . The culture of an internat is the central component of its reclaiming (changing) ability, and the most important part of this culture is the internat's ideology or Unifying Theme. (Wozner, 1991, p. 33)

A significant difference between the framework developed in the current study and Wozner's is the method used to generate them. Whereas the current study utilized the grounded theory approach involving extensive data gathering within a purposive sample of homes, Wozner drew upon a number of studies, preexisting frameworks, and theoretical orientations as well as his extensive professional experience in the broad field of residential care (Wozner, 1991, p. xiii). While it would not be fair or accurate to say that Wozner's study was not "grounded," it is clear that it was grounded in a very different way than the current study. Therefore, it is interesting to assess the commonalities and the differences in the resulting theoretical frameworks.

First, both studies resulted in visual depictions of the frameworks. Wozner labels his a "schema" whereas the current study refers to a "matrix." In fact, both involve matrices. The Wozner matrix or schema consists of a two dimensional rectangle with two axes, one depicting a continuum of "total" to "partial" regulation of an individual's life-space, and the other depicting a continuum of "autocracy" to "democracy" indicating the degree of participation by the "internees" in the ongoing life and work of the internat.

Also central to the Wozner framework is a basic principle of making the internat experience rewarding for the members (Wozner, 1991, p. 35). This principle can be seen to encompass the central theme discovered in the group home study as well as aspects of the major psychosocial processes as well. That is, group home residents need to experience a sense of normality through the responsiveness of the staff members who are seen to be acting congruently in service of the resident's best interests.

Second, the Wozner framework identifies seven domains of an internat, including:

Domain 1. The internees by themselves.
Domain 2. The internees and the staff.
Domain 3. The staff by themselves.
Domain 4. The staff and the environment.
Domain 5. The environment by itself.
Domain 6. The internees and the environment.
Domain 7. The internees, the staff and the environment.

It is evident that these domains parallel the levels and interactions between levels outlined in the current group home study framework. One of the major differences is that the analysis of staff members in the group home framework is broken down into three levels: managers, supervisors, and careworkers. In addition, the Wozner approach refers to "a *motivating interaction system* in which the members progress toward given goals" (Wozner, 1991, p. 47, emphasis in original). Two additional sets of constructs are required to complete the matrix of "quality of life subsystems" (Wozner, 1991, p. 48). One is termed "fields" and the other is termed "modes."

The "modes" of functioning consist of the expressive, adaptive, integrative and conservative modes. The expressive mode consists of events which originate within the internat (or the individual) and are actualized outside the internat (or the individual). For example, social and cultural activities involving the fulfillment of personal choices related to actions and activities beyond the internat are within this mode. The adaptation mode consists of events that originate outside the internat (or the individual) and are actualized outside the internat (or the individual). Such events can be characterized as more consuming than fulfilling activities.

The integrative mode concerns events originating within the internat (or the individual) and are actualized within the internat (or the individual). This mode relates primarily to the health and balance within the internee's life and "includes the congruence of the various components of the internat as an organization and the co-operation of the various members" (Wozner, 1991, pp. 48-49). The fourth mode, the conservative function, consists of events which have originated outside of the internat (or the individual) and are actualized inside the internat. This mode relates to identity, genetic makeup, physical structure, and cultural roots.

These four modes of functioning are then broken down into subsets by the four "fields of functioning." The fields of functioning include the psychological-personal, physical-behavioral, social/societal, and cultural. By juxtaposing the four modes with the four fields, sixteen subsets (boxes) are created that Wozner refers to as the quality of internat life subsets map (Wozner, 1991, p. 50). This map is then used as a structure for analyzing the elements and functioning of the internat environment across the seven previously described domains and addressing six stages of intervention. The six stages of intervention identified are similar to a case planning model and include problem definition, outcome setting, information gathering, alternative selection, execution, and outcome evaluation. Finally, each analytical subset (box) in the framework has a central principle defined. For example, box 1 in domain 1 (the internees by themselves), is called "How to Motivate the Internees to Learn," and the accompanying principle is "The implementation of rewards for good study habits improves learning" (Wozner, 1991, p. 79).

One of the features of the Wozner framework that will have been noted by the reader is its complexity. Several different theoretical models have been adapted and juxtaposed in a manner that requires considerable study, that does not use everyday language, and that is difficult to keep in one's mind for ongoing use. It is a rather formal and technical framework with a behavioral orientation that might prove useful to the more technically minded managers and evaluators. However, it is not likely to be used on a moment-by-moment or even regular basis by front-line workers or their immediate supervisors. On the other hand, the group home framework has been developed using everyday language and appears more readily accessible to careworkers, and it is more conducive to internalization and use in practice on an ongoing basis.

Overall, both frameworks seek to isolate specific elements and processes within the rather bewildering life and life-space of residential settings and to offer a theoretical and analytical tool for understanding and enhancing practice. Time will tell whether either framework will be successful in influencing practice beyond the direct scope of influence of their developers.

SUMMARY

On the basis of a selected review of the residential child and youth care literatures in both the United Kingdom and North America, the present study appears to be the first to present the findings of a major grounded theory study of residential group care for children and youth. Further, it is one of only a handful of studies identified that were initiated with the primary aim of developing a detailed and comprehensive theoretical framework for analyzing and guiding practice.

As stated at the beginning of this study, it was hoped that the grounded theory framework emerging from this research process would offer assistance in identifying and putting into an integrated perspective some of the major foci for practice, training, management, supervision, policy development and further research in residential group care. The comparisons made in this chapter with ten relevant studies would suggest that the present framework both complements and extends in some provocative ways the findings of other studies in this area. The final chapter will consider possible implications of this theoretical framework for new directions in group home policy, education, practice and research.

Chapter 9

Implications for New Directions in Child and Youth Care Policy Development, Education, Practice, and Research

We must work tenaciously for change. We've been lulled into accepting systems without looking into the human faces that are impacted by them. These real, hurting people cry out for us to think deeply and creatively regarding our orientation towards families and the child welfare system.

–John Seita, Martin Mitchell, and Christi Tobin (1996, p. 135)

This chapter includes implications of the framework developed in this study for new directions that could be pursued by those involved in child and youth care policy development, education, practice and research.

CHILD AND YOUTH CARE POLICY

For policy makers, the relevance and use of this framework would probably be assessed in terms of the framework's ability to offer guidance in relation to two questions:

1. Is there a unique role for group homes within the child and youth care service system such that they should receive ongoing support?
2. What should be the major foci of legislation, standards of practice, and policy development in relation to group home care?

While both of these questions can be addressed in a preliminary way here, the true test will come only when the study is made widely available to those charged with making policy decisions concerning child and youth care ser-

[Haworth co-indexing entry note]: "Implications for New Directions in Child and Youth Care Policy Development, Education, Practice, and Research." Anglin, James P. Co-published simultaneously in *Child & Youth Services* (The Haworth Press, Inc.) Vol. 24, No. 1/2, 2002, pp. 153-163; and: *Pain, Normality, and the Struggle for Congruence: Reinterpreting Residential Care for Children and Youth* (James P. Anglin) The Haworth Press, Inc., 2002, pp. 153-163. Single or multiple copies of this article are available for a fee from The Haworth Document Delivery Service [1-800-HAWORTH, 9:00 a.m. - 5:00 p.m. (EST). E-mail address: docdelivery@haworthpress.com].

http://www.haworthpress.com/store/product.asp?sku=J024
10.1300/J024v24n01_10

vices and residential care. However, the framework and some of the findings have been presented at the national Child Welfare 2000 Conference (Anglin, 2000) attended by policy makers from across Canada as well as through a national teleconference (Child Welfare League of Canada, 2001a). As a result of these presentations, consultations in three provinces (New Brunswick, Manitoba, and British Columbia) and the Yukon Territory (Anglin, 2001b) have been undertaken by the author in relation to residential group home care.

One of the major messages of this research study that appears to attract the attention of policy makers is its finding that there is a positive and unique role for group homes in the system of care, and that the features that differentiate this form of care from traditional foster care can be identified and specified. Specifically, the seven characteristics of group homes outlined in Chapter 5 in relation to the needs and preferences of youth are seen as helpful in situating group home care in the overall system of care for young people. A second aspect of the framework that appears to attract the interest of policy makers is its "intuitive grab" in terms of its identified components and processes as well as its focus on aspects of group home life and group home work that seems to get to the heart of the enterprise in a relevant, useful and meaningful manner.

Specifically, in terms of implications for agency level policy development and management, this study suggests that the major foci of policy should include (a) standards of practice that support the achievement of congruence throughout an agency and group home organization, and (b) appropriate pre-service education, in-house training, and ongoing supervision that address the major psychosocial processes identified in the framework.

Further, using the overall framework as an assessment tool, the congruence of a home can be analyzed both within and across the five levels of operation, thereby assisting with both the assessment and potential intervention to enhance group home functioning. It is interesting to note that, after this framework had been developed, it was pointed out that the three core psychosocial processes discovered in this study closely parallel the three primary domains identified as three sides of an equilateral triangle in an assessment framework emerging from the Social Care Group of the Department of Health in the United Kingdom: family and environmental factors ("creating an extrafamilial living environment"), parenting capacity ("responding to pain and pain-based behavior"), and child's developmental needs ("developing a sense of normality") (Department of Health, 2000, p. 89).

The policy and procedural infrastructure necessary for supporting the staff in a group home to respond effectively to psychoemotional pain and the related pain-based behavior of youth and to deal with their own secondary pain and anxiety should also be important concerns for policy makers, especially in the current climate of heightened sensitivity to issues of risk management and vicarious liability as a result of recent court decisions (Anglin, 2000). Governments are increasingly being held accountable for any abusive or inappropriate behavior occurring in group homes operated under their authority, whether under contract or directly operated.

CHILD AND YOUTH CARE EDUCATION

Educators will be interested to know whether this framework reveals new insights into the education and training needs of the various role players involved in the provision of residential group care and to what degree their teaching curricula may need to be modified. Specifically, the major education-related questions would likely include:

1. Do the current curricula for child and youth care workers prepare them (a) to create a living environment that supports youth in developing a sense of normality, (b) to respond effectively to pain and pain-based behavior (both the residents' and their own) in the residential context, and (c) to demonstrate the eleven key interactional dynamics in a manner that supports the attainment of congruence in service of the children's best interests within a residential setting?
2. Do the curricula for supervisors and managers prepare them for the task of being "supportively challenging" within a framework for creating an extrafamilial living environment that consistently and coherently serves the children's best interests? Further, are they being prepared to model and facilitate the eleven key interactional dynamics both within their management relationships and across the levels of the organization?
3. Does more need to be done in order to make appropriate education and training more accessible to prospective and existing residential workers, and should a much larger percentage of residential group care staff be formally qualified and certified as competent to carry out this complex and demanding work?

It is difficult to provide specific answers to these questions without a detailed program-by-program curriculum review. Recently, however, two major initiatives aimed at defining frameworks for developing and assessing curricula for child and youth care work have been undertaken on both sides of the Atlantic Ocean. In North America, the Association for Child and Youth Care Practice (2001) has issued a set of draft competencies, while in the United Kingdom, the Quality Assurance Agency for Higher Education (2000) has defined a set of benchmark statements for Social Work, including "child care" and "group-care." There is no separate profession in the United Kingdom comparable to Child and Youth Care in North America or to the Social Pedagogue or Educateur in the rest of the European Community. Both of these documents will now be reviewed, beginning with the North American competencies.

The North American Certification Project (Association for Child and Youth Care Practice, 2001) has distributed for consultation the document *Proposed Competencies for Professional Child and Youth Work Personnel* that outlines a proposed competency framework and a detailed set of practice competencies as the potential basis for certification efforts for child and youth care practitioners at the provincial and state levels throughout Canada and the United States. A review of this competency document indicates that it has been designed for the first professional level of certification, and important aspects of all three major psychosocial processes identified within the current group home framework are addressed, directly or indirectly, in the document. In addition, the eleven interactional dynamics are also well-represented, and the five levels of organizational operation are recognized. Examples of provisions from the *Competency* document are provided below in relation to the specific elements of this study's framework that are provided in italics. These examples are offered for illustrative purposes only and are not intended to represent a comprehensive analysis of the entire document.

Psychosocial Processes

I. Creating an extrafamilial living environment

- "design and implement programs and planned environments";
- "provide an environment that celebrates the array of human diversity";
- "create and maintain a safe and growth promoting environment";
- "describe the messages conveyed by the environment."

II. Responding to pain and pain-based behavior

- "describe own needs and feelings and keep them in perspective when professionally engaged";
- "recognize own strengths and limitations, feelings and needs";
- "incorporate 'wellness' practices into own lifestyle."

III. Developing a sense of normality

- "evaluate the developmental appropriateness of environments for meeting the individual needs of clients";
- "develop and maintain relationships with community members and neighbors to identify community standards and expectations of behavior";
- "well maintained clothing that reflects the age and cultural/human diversity of the child."

Interactional Dynamics

a. Listening and responding with respect

- "help clarify the meaning of that communication";
- "set appropriate boundaries and limits on the behavior using clear and respectful communication."

· b. Communicating a framework for understanding

- "state a philosophy of practice that provides guiding principles for the design, delivery and management of services."

c. Building rapport and relationship

- "identify and demonstrate the personal characteristics that foster and support relationship development."

d. Establishing structure, routine, and expectations

- "employ developmentally sensitive expectations in setting appropriate boundaries and limits";
- "use structures, routines, and activities to promote effective relationships."

e. Inspiring commitment

- "employ genuine relationships to promote positive behavior";
- "build cohesion among team members."

f. Offering emotional and developmental support

- "support development in a broad range of circumstances in different domains and contexts";
- "develop relationships with service recipients that are caring, purposeful, goal-directed, and rehabilitative in nature."

g. Challenging thinking and action

- "design and implement challenging age, developmentally, and cultural and human diversity appropriate activity programs."

h. Sharing power and decision making

- "providing for the participation of children/youth and families in the planning, implementation, and evaluation of service impacting them";
- "promote clients [sic] participation in activity planning."

i. Respecting personal space and time

- "involve clients in space design, and maintenance."

j. Discovering and uncovering potential

- "assist the clients in identifying and developing their strengths through activities and other experiences."

k. Providing resources

- "select and obtain resources necessary to conduct a particular activity or activity program";
- "support family in gaining resources for interests, education, and the like";
- "give accurate developmental information in a manner that facilitates growth."

Levels of Home Operation

1. Extra-agency

- "sustain collaborative relations with other organizations and persons."

2. Management

- "translate agency mission and group objectives into individual treatment . . . plans."

3. Supervision

- "communication with a supervisor"

4. Carework/teamwork

- "establish and maintain effective relationships with a team environment."

5. Youth and family

- "encourage children and families to share folklore and traditions."

The document, *The Proposed Competencies for Professional Child and Youth Work Personnel* (Association for Child and Youth Care Practice, 2001), reflects a general acknowledgement in the North American child and youth care field of most of the elements of the framework constructed in this study. While the core theme of "congruence" and the major psychosocial processes of "creating an extrafamilial living environment," "responding to pain and pain-based behavior" and "developing a sense of normality" are not explicitly acknowledged, the eleven interactional dynamics and five levels of agency and home operation are addressed. Understandably, given the purpose of the document as a certification framework for direct practice, more emphasis is placed on the carework function than on extra-agency relations, management or supervision.

What this study's framework can add to the *Competency* document is a more explicit and focused identification of how the specific competencies will need to be implemented through the major interactional and psychosocial processes characteristic of the residential care environment. The *Competency* document recognizes that "organizing the competencies within the contexts of practice will be a future project" (Association for Child and Youth Care Practice, 2001, p. 6). It is suggested that this study's theoretical framework might well serve as an organizing framework for an analysis of these competencies in relation to residential group care.

The Quality Assurance Agency for Higher Education (2000) benchmark statements are much more general than the North American competency provisions, and they encompass a much broader range of issues than child and youth care work. In fact, "child care" (p. 3) and "group-care" (p. 14) are only briefly mentioned in the document. Such broad statements as the following address a number of the aspects of this study's theoretical framework:

- "help people to gain, regain or maintain control of their own affairs . . .";
- "the contribution of different approaches to management, leadership and quality in public and independent human services."
- "employ understanding of human agency at macro (societal), mezzo (organisational and community) and micro (inter- and intra-personal) levels";
- "build and sustain purposeful relationships with people . . .";
- "manage the complex dynamics of dependency, and, in some settings, provide direct care and personal support in every day living situations";
- "listen actively to others, engage appropriately with the life experiences of service users, understand accurately their viewpoint and overcome personal prejudices to respond appropriately to a range of complex personal and interpersonal situations";
- "involve users of social work services in ways that increase their resources, capacity and power to influence factors affecting their lives";
- "act within a framework of multiple accountability . . .";
- "challenge others when necessary, in ways that are most likely to produce positive outcomes."

While the benchmarks do not contradict the elements articulated within the group home study's framework, there is not the level of detail nor the focus on child and youth care practice characteristic of the North American competency document. Therefore, in order to construct a curriculum designed to address the needs of group home workers specifically, the benchmark statements would need to be adapted and written in a finer grained manner with the specific psychosocial processes, interactional dynamics, and levels of home operation characteristic of group care settings more fully acknowledged.

CHILD AND YOUTH CARE PRACTICE

For practitioners, the main test of the proposed framework would likely focus on questions such as the following:

1. Does this framework adequately reflect the reality that I have come to know?
2. How does this framework help me to better understand this reality?
3. How will this framework help me to practice more effectively?

These questions speak to several issues in the group home study: the adequacy of the research sample; the degree to which the language and categories of the framework remain explicitly grounded in the sample data; the fit, relevance and utility of the framework itself; and the perceived significance and "grab" of the new insights offered by the framework.

Several presentations of this framework to residential child and youth care practitioners, managers, and policy makers, and the ensuing questions and dialogue appear to offer evidence of significant "grab" and relevance. Presentations at the Child Welfare 2000 national research symposium (Anglin, 2000) and the Child Welfare League of Canada teleconference (Anglin, 2001a) have resulted in several further opportunities by invitation, including a full-day forum for almost one hundred residential child and youth care providers from all levels of group home operation in New Brunswick, a presentation to the System of Care Working Group in the Ministry of Children and Family Development (Ministry of Children and Family Development, 2002), and a public review of group homes for children and youth for the Minister of Health and Social Service in the Yukon Territory (Anglin, 2001b).

At the Child Welfare 2000 symposium, the presentation of the findings of this study were prefaced with a comment in support of foster care and foster carers. A number of provincial foster care association presidents and board members were present, and there was a danger that they would interpret the identification of some of the strengths of group homes as an attack on foster homes. Despite this precaution, one of the foster carers did feel offended by what she perceived as criticism of her ability to care for challenging youth. However, on the day after the presentation and in a personal follow-up discussion, she approached the author to say that she had thought about the issue of the intensity of intimacy, and she now appreciated the fact that she may have unwittingly placed unnecessary pressure on some youth placed with her with the intention of "giving them" a family that she had thought that these youth needed. Thus, in the end, the framework proved useful to this foster parent as well as to participants more directly involved in group home management who demonstrated interest by requesting additional materials and consultations.

The Child Welfare League of Canada teleconference drew 285 participants, received positive evaluations for its relevance and usefulness, and engendered much lively discussion as well as invitations to offer several workshops and presentations to provincial and territorial committees. While there is some initial evidence of the "grab, fit, relevance, and utility" of the framework for practitioners and managers at various operational levels, the questions proposed at the start of this section will be better and more fully answered when this study is published and thus made available for critique and possible application by a much wider range of residential group care practitioners.

In the final stages of writing up this framework, the Framework for the Assessment of Children in Need and Their Families (Department of Health, 2000) was brought to the author's attention, and it was intriguing to note how closely the three domains proposed for assessment paralleled the three psychosocial processes identified in this group home study. The three assessment domains and three core psychosocial processes identified are juxtaposed below, demonstrating the parallels related to the created environment, caregivers' responses and the child's development.

Assessment Domains	Psychosocial Processes
family and environmental factors	creating an extrafamilial living environment
parenting capacity	responding to pain and pain-based behavior
child's developmental needs	developing a sense of normality

The Department of Health (2000) assessment framework document describes the three domains as "inter-related systems" (p. 18) and urges that "the complex interplay of factors across all three domains should be carefully understood and analysed" (p. 25). Further, the document states that the use of this framework "increases the likelihood of parents and children experiencing consistency between professionals and themselves about what will be important for children's wellbeing and healthy development" (p. x). Thus, both the group home study's framework and the Department of Health assessment framework also share an emphasis on the importance of consistency, or congruence, for ensuring children's well-being and healthy development. However, the two studies were undertaken for very different purposes, thereby rendering further detailed comparison of the frameworks not very fruitful in relation to the foci of this analysis.

CHILD AND YOUTH CARE RESEARCH

For researchers, the main test of the framework may include questions such as:

1. Does this framework help to give new shape or new meaning to the findings of existing research in any significant way?
2. Does this framework provide a useful and promising guide for further research?

The first of these two questions was addressed to a significant degree in the previous chapter through a selective review of relevant residential care texts from the United Kingdom and North America. Briefly, the analysis in the previous chapter, this study, and its resulting framework appear to provide complementary evidence for some existing notions (for example, the significance of congruence in ensuring a well-functioning home) as well as some provocative insights into possible blind spots in the literature (for example, the significance of psychoemotional pain and pain-based behavior). Overall, it would appear that the current framework may offer a succinct, relevant and useful analytical tool that could potentially assist the role players at all levels in the children and youth residential care sector where few such frameworks seem to exist.

In relation to the framework's potential to guide future research, one doctoral student has already utilized elements of the framework to structure a review of recent residential care literature and has found that the eleven interactional dynamics stood up well as an analytical framework for analyzing the literature in relation to practice-based issues. In addition, the author has used the framework to undertake an evaluation study of a complex residential program, and it has proven effective in both structuring the evaluation and in communicating the findings and their implications for organizational change to both agency and government personnel.

Once again, however, the true test will come when the framework is published, academically critiqued and considered for use by others in helping to frame future research inquiries.

CONCLUSION

This research study of staffed group home life and work with children and youth was undertaken in order to construct a framework for understanding and practice. It is hoped that the resulting framework matrix and its identified elements and dynamics will assist individuals, agencies, and government departments committed to providing good residential group home care to the young people who need it.

As stated earlier in this document, if a service such as group home care is to be utilized, then we need to know how, when and for whom it can best be used, and value it as a *positive choice* in these circumstances. A service that is not valued, or that is considered always to be an unsatisfactory or second-rate option will inevitably deteriorate and will ultimately reflect these self-fulfilling expectations. Our young people are asking for and deserve the best group homes that we can provide.

References

Agnew, N. M. & Pyke, S. W. (1982). *The science game: An introduction to research in the behavioral sciences*. Englewood Cliffs, NJ: Prentice-Hall.

Aichhorn, A. (1935). *Wayward youth*. New York: Viking.

Ainsworth, F. & Fulcher, L. C. (Eds.). (1981). *Group care for children: Concepts and issues*. London: Tavistock.

Ainsworth, M. D. (1972). Attachment and dependency: A comparison. In J. S. Geriwitz, (Ed.), *Attachment and dependency* (pp. 97-136). Washington, DC: Winston.

Ainsworth, M. D., Bell, B. M. & Stayton, D. (1974). Infant-mother attachment and social development: Socialization as a product of reciprocal responsiveness to signals. In M. P. Richard (Ed.), *The integration of a child into a social world* (pp. 99-135). Cambridge, England: Cambridge University Press.

Alasuutari, P. (1995). *Researching culture: Qualitative method and cultural studies*. London: Sage.

Alaszewski, A. (1986). Literature review: Performance and inspection in the social services. *British Journal of Social Work, 16*, 679-688.

Alston, P. (Ed.). (1994). *The best interests of the child: Reconciling culture and human rights*. Oxford: Clarendon.

American Heritage Dictionary. (1970). New York: Houghton Mifflin.

Anglin, J. P. (1984). Counselling a single parent and child: Functional and dysfunctional patterns of communication. *Journal of Child and Youth Care, 2*(2), 33-45.

Anglin, J. P. (1985). Parent education: Can an old tradition address new needs and new realities? *Family Strengths VI*, 203-226.

Anglin, J. P. (1991). Residential care for children and youth in Canada. In M. Gottesman (1991), *Residential child care: An international reader* (pp. 48-62). London: Whiting and Birch.

Anglin, J. P. (1992). Children's rights and the magic beanstock. *Journal of Emotional and Behavioral Problems, 1*(3), 36-39.

Anglin, J. P. (1994). Canada: New trends, new perspectives, radical changes. In M. Gottesman (Ed.), *Recent changes and new trends in extrafamilial child care: An international perspective* (pp. 24-30). London: Whiting and Birch.

Anglin, J. P. (1998). "Constructing an account of residential care and residential life of children and youth: An outline of a research proposal." Unpublished. School of Child and Youth Care, University of Victoria.

Anglin, J. P. (2000). *Meaning and implication of the move to paramountcy of the safety and well-being of the child in child welfare legislation*. Ottawa: Justice Canada.

Anglin, J. P. (2001a). *Staffed group homes for children and youth: Understanding their role and ensuring quality*. National Teleconference Transcript, February 10. Ottawa: Child Welfare League of Canada.

Anglin, J. P. (2001b). *Their future begins today: Yukon residential care report*. Whitehorse: Department of Health and Social Services, Yukon Government.

Anglin, J. P. & Working Group. (1978). Residential child care programming: Standards and guidelines; Chapter VII. In *Children's residential care facilities: Proposed standards and guidelines.* Toronto: Children's Services Division, Ministry of Community and Social Services.

Arieli, M., Kashti, Y. & Shlasky, S. (1983). *Living at school: Israeli residential schools as people-processing organizations.* Tel Aviv: Ramot Publishing.

Artz, S. (1994). *Feeling as a way of knowing: A practical guide for working with emotional experience.* Toronto: Trifolium Books.

Association for Child and Youth Care Practice. (2001). *Proposed competencies for professional child and youth work personnel.* (Draft). [Electronic version]. Retrieved August 30, 2001 from <http://www.acycp.org>.

Bandura, A. (1977). *Social learning theory.* Englewood Cliffs, NJ: Prentice-Hall.

Barnes, F. H. (1986). Comment on Soth. *Child Care Quarterly, 15*(2), 121-123.

Barnes, F. H. (1991). From warehouse to greenhouse: Play, work and the routines of daily living in groups as the core of milieu treatment. In J. Beker & Z. Eisikovits (Eds.), *Knowledge utilization in residential child and youth care practice* (pp. 123-155). Washington, DC: Child Welfare League of America.

Barnes, F. H. & Kelman, S. H. (1974). From slogan to concepts: A basis for change in child care work. *Child Care Quarterly, 3*(1), 7-23.

Barret, M. C. & McKelvey, J. (1980). Stresses and strains on the child care worker: Typologies for assessment. *Child Welfare, 59*(5), 277-285.

Beker, J. & Eisikovits, Z. (Eds.). (1991). *Knowledge utilization in residential child and youth care practice.* Washington, DC: Child Welfare League of America.

Beker, J. & Magnuson, D. (Eds.). (1996). *Residential education as an option for at-risk youth.* New York: Haworth.

Belenky, M. F., Clinchy, B. M., Goldberger, N. R. & Tarule, J. M. (1986). *Women's ways of knowing: The development of self, voice and mind.* New York: Basic Books.

Benner, P. (1984). *From novice to expert: Excellence and power in clinical nursing practice.* Menlo Park, CA: Addison-Wesley.

Benner, P. & Wrubel, J. (1989). *The primacy of caring: Stress and coping in health and illness.* Menlo Park, CA: Addison-Wesley.

Bensman, J. & Lilienfeld, R. (1973). *Craft and consciousness.* New York: John Wiley.

Berkley, G. E. (1980). *The craft of public administration.* Boston: Allyn & Bacon.

Berridge, D. (1985). *Children's homes.* Oxford: Blackwell.

Berridge, D. & Brodie, I. (1998). *Children's homes revisited.* London: Jessica Kingsley.

Bettelheim, B. (1950). *Love is not enough.* New York: Free Press.

Bettelheim, B. (1955). *Truants from life.* New York: Free Press.

Bettelheim, B. (1967). *The empty fortress.* New York: Free Press.

Bettelheim, B. (1974). *A home for the heart.* London: Thames and Hudson.

Bettelheim, B. (1988). *A good enough parent.* New York: Vintage Books.

Bloom, R.B. (1992). When staff members sexually abuse children in residential care. *Child Welfare, 71*(2), 131-145.

Blumer, H. (1969). *Symbolic interactionism: Perspective and method.* Berkeley: University of California Press.

Boone, L. (1999, October 7). *More options* [Letter to the editor, editorial page] *Times-Colonist*, Victoria, British Columbia.

Bowlby, J. (1958). The nature of the child's tie to its mother. *International Journal of Psychoanalysis, 39*, 350-373.

Bowlby, J. (1969). *Attachment and loss*, Volumes I and II. London: Hogarth Press.

Brendtro, L.K. & Ness, A.E. (1983). *Re-educating troubled youth: Environments for teaching and treatment*. New York: Aldine de Gruyter.

British Columbia Royal Commission of Family and Children's Law. (1975). *Fifth report: The protection of children (child care)*. Vancouver: Province of British Columbia.

Bronfenbrenner, U. (1979). *The ecology of human development*. Cambridge, MA: Harvard University Press.

Brown, E., Bullock, R., Hobson, C. & Little, M. (1998). *Making residential care work: Structure and culture in children's homes*. Aldershot: Ashgate.

Brown, R.A. & Hill, B.A. (1996). Opportunity for change: Exploring an alternative to residential treatment. *Child Welfare, 75*(1), 35-57.

Buckholdt, D. R. & Gubrium, J. (1979). *Caretakers: Treating emotionally disturbed children*. London: Sage.

Bullock, R., Gooch, D. & Little, M. (1998). *Children going home: The reunification of families*. Aldershot: Ashgate.

Bullock, R., Little, M. & Millham, S. (1993*). Residential care for children: A review of the research*. London: HMSO.

Burford, G. E. & Fulcher, L. C. (1985). Team functioning in group care. In F. Ainsworth & L. C. Fulcher (Eds.), *Group care practice with children* (pp. 187-214). London, England: Tavistock.

Burmeister, E. (1960). *The professional houseparent*. New York: Columbia University Press.

Canadian Council on Children and Youth. (1978). *Admittance restricted: The child as citizen in Canada*. Ottawa: CCSD Publication.

Caplan, N. (1975). *The use of social knowledge in policy decision at the national level*. Ann Arbor, MI: Institute for Social Research, University of Michigan.

Cassam, E. & Gupta, H. (1992). *Quality assurance for social care agencies: A practical guide*. London: Longman.

Chenitz, W. C. & Swanson, J. M. (1986). *From practice to grounded theory: Qualitative research in nursing*. Menlo Park, CA: Addison-Wesley.

Chrisjohn, R. & Young, S. (1997). *The circle game: Shadows and substance in the Indian residential school experience in Canada*. Penticton, BC: Theytus Books.

Cliffe, D. & Berridge, D. (1992). *Closing children's homes*. London: National Children's Bureau.

Clough, R. (1982). *Residential work*. London: Macmillan Press.

Clough, R. (2000). *The practice of residential work*. London: Macmillan Press.

Coates, R. B., Miller, A. D. & Ohlin, L. (1978). *Diversity in a youth correctional system: Handling delinquents in Massachusetts*. Cambridge, MA: Ballinger.

Collins, D. & Colorado, P. (1988). Native culture and child care services. In G. Charles & P. Gabor, P. (Eds.), *Issues in child and youth care practice in Alberta* (pp. 83-94). Lethbridge, Alberta: Lethbridge Community College.

Colton, M.J. (1988). Foster and residential care practices compared. *British Journal of Social Work, 18*, 25-42.

Commission on Emotional and Learning Disorders in Children. (1970). *One million children–The CELDIC report.* Toronto: Leonard Crainford.

Courtioux, M., Davies Jones, H., Kalcher, J., Steinhauser, W., Tuggener, H. & Waaldijk, K. (1985). *The socialpedagogue in Europe: Living with others as a profession.* Zurich: University of Zurich.

Davis, L. (1987). *Rivers of pain, bridges of hope.* Hong Kong: Writers' and Publishers' Cooperative. (Distributed in the United Kingdom by the Social Care Association).

Denholm, C., Ferguson, R. V. & Pence, A. (Eds.). (1993). *Professional child and youth care* (Second Edition). Vancouver: University of British Columbia Press.

Department of Health. (1991). *Children in the public care: A review of residential care.* (The Utting Report). London: HMSO.

Department of Health. (1998). *Caring for children away from home: Messages from research.* London: HMSO.

Department of Health. (2000). *Framework for the assessment of children in need and their families.* London: The Stationery Office.

Durrant, M. (1993). *Residential treatment: A cooperative, competency-based approach to therapy and program design.* New York: W.W. Norton & Company.

Eichler, M. (1983). *Families in Canada today. Recent changes and their policy consequences.* Toronto: Gage.

Eisikovits, R. (1983). No exit: Residential treatment and the "sick role" trap. *Child Care Quarterly, 12,* 36-44.

Eisikovits, Z. & Beker, J. (1983). Beyond professionalism: The child and youth care worker as craftsman. *Child Care Quarterly, 12*(2), 93-120.

Eisikovits, Z. & Beker, J. (Eds.). (1986). *Residential care in community context: Insights from the Israeli experience.* New York: Haworth Press.

Erikson, E. H. (1950). *Childhood and society.* New York: Norton.

Fanshel, D. & Shinn, E. (1978). *Children in foster care.* New York: Columbia University Press.

Farmer, E. & Pollock, S. (1998). *Sexually abused and abusing children in substitute care.* Chichester: Wiley.

Fewster, G. & Garfat, T. (1993). Residential child and youth care. In C. Denholm, R. V. Ferguson & A. Pence (Eds.), *Professional child and youth care in Canada* (pp. 15-43) (Second Edition). Vancouver: UBC Press.

Fournier, S. & Crey, E. (1997). *Stolen from our embrace: The abduction of First Nations children and the restoration of aboriginal communities.* Toronto: Douglas & McIntyre.

Fox Harding, L. (1991). *Perspectives in child care policy.* London: Longman.

Frost, N., Mills, S. & Stein, M. (1999). *Understanding residential child care.* Aldershot: Ashgate.

Fulcher, L. C. & Ainsworth, F. (Eds.). (1985). *Group care practice with children.* London: Tavistock.

Garbarino, J. (Ed.). (1982). *Children and families in the social environment.* New York: Aldine.

Glaser, B. (1978). *Theoretical sensitivity.* Mill Valley, CA: Sociology Press.

Glaser, B. (1992). *Basics of grounded theory analysis.* Mill Valley, CA: Sociology Press.

Glaser, B. (Ed.). (1993). *Examples of grounded theory: A reader.* Mill Valley, CA: Sociology Press.

Glaser, B. (Ed.). (1994). *More grounded theory methodology: A reader.* Mill Valley, CA: Sociology Press.

Glaser, B. (1998). *Doing grounded theory: Issues and discussions.* Mill Valley, CA: Sociology Press.

Glaser, B. G. & Strauss, A. L. (1967). *The discovery of grounded theory.* Chicago, IL: Aldine.

Goffman, E. (1961). *Asylums.* Chicago: Aldine.

Goldstein, J., Freud, A. & Solnit, A. J. (1973). *Beyond the best interests of the child.* New York: Free Press.

Goldstein, J., Freud, A. & Solnit, A.J. (1979). *Before the best interests of the child.* New York: Free Press.

Goocher, B. E. (1996). Where do we go from here?: Building on Shealy's work. *Child and Youth Care Forum, 25*(5), 281-283.

Gottesman, M. (Ed.). (1991). *Residential child care: An international reader.* London: Whiting and Birch.

Gottesman, M. (Ed.). (1994). *Recent changes and new trends in extrafamilial child care: An international perspective.* London: Whiting and Birch.

Gove, T. J. (1995a). *Report of the Gove inquiry into child protection. Volume 1: Matthew's story.* British Columbia: Ministry of Social Services.

Gove, T. J. (1995b). *Report of the Gove inquiry into child protection. Volume 2: Matthew's legacy.* British Columbia: Ministry of Social Services.

Gove, T. J. (1995c). *Report of the Gove inquiry into child protection. Volume 3: Executive summary.* British Columbia: Ministry of Social Services.

Haig-Brown, C. (1988). *Resistance and renewal: Surviving the Indian residential school.* Vancouver: Tillacum Library.

Hepworth, P. (1975). *Residential services for children in Canada.* Personal social services in Canada: A review; Volume 4. Ottawa: Canadian Council on Social Development.

Heshusius, L. & Ballard, K. (Eds.). (1996). *From positivism to interpretivism and beyond: Tales of transformation in educational and social research.* New York: Teachers College Press.

Hills, D. & Child, C. (2000). *Leadership in residential care: Evaluating qualification training.* Chichester: Wiley.

Hobbs, N. (1974). Helping disturbed children: Psychological and ecological strategies. In M. Wolins (Ed.), *Successful group care: Exploration in the powerful environment.* Chicago, IL: Aldine.

Hobbs, N. (1982). *The troubled and troubling child.* San Francisco, CA: Jossey-Bass.

Hunt, D.E. (1987). *Beginning with ourselves: In practice, theory and human affairs.* Cambridge, MA: Brookline Books.

Kahan, B. (1994). *Growing up in groups.* London: HMSO.

Kimball, S.T. & Partridge, W.L. (1979). *The craft of community study: Fieldwork dialogues.* University of Florida Social Science Monographs, No. 65. Gainesville: University Presses of Florida.

Konopka, G. (1970). *Group work in the institution: A modern challenge.* New York: Association Press.

Kuhn, T. (1962). *The structure of scientific revolutions.* Chicago: University of Chicago Press.

Lasson, I. (1981). *Where's my mum?* Birmingham: Pepar Publications.

Levy, A. & Kahan, B. (1991). *The pindown experience and the protection of children: The report of the Staffordshire child care inquiry.* Banbury, England: Cheney and Sons.

Levy, Z. (1993). *Negotiating positive identity in a group care community.* New York: Haworth.

Levy, Z. (1996). Conceptual foundations of developmentally oriented residential education: A holistic framework for group care that works. In J. Beker & D. Magnuson (Eds.), *Residential education as an option for at-risk youth* (pp. 69-83). New York: Haworth.

Lincoln, Y. S. & Guba, G. E. (1985). *Naturalistic inquiry.* Beverly Hills: Sage.

Little, M. & Kelly, S. (1995). *Life without problems? The achievements of a therapeutic community.* Aldershot: Arena.

MacMurray, J. (1957). *The self as agent: Being the Gifford lectures delivered in the University of Glasgow in 1953.* London: Faber and Faber.

Magnusson, W. (Ed.). (1984). *The new reality: The politics of restraint in British Columbia.* Vancouver: New Star Books.

Maier, H. W. (1979). The core of care: The essential ingredients for the development of children at home and away from home. *Child Care Quarterly, 8,* 161-173.

Maier, H. W. (1981). Essential components in care and treatment environments for children and youth. In F. Ainsworth, & L. C. Fulcher (Eds.), *Group care for children: Concepts and issues* (pp. 19-70). London: Tavistock.

Maier, H. W., Greenwald, M., Kelly, C. S., Klassen, T., Krueger, M. A., Pratt, S., Rose, L. & VanderVen, K. (1995). *Child and Youth Care Forum, 24*(4), 269-278.

Marland, M. (1975). *The craft of the classroom.* Exeter, NH: Heinemann Educational Books.

Mattingly, M. A. (1977). Sources of stress and burnout professional child care work. *Child Care Quarterly, 6*(2), 127-137.

McCann, J. B. & James, A. (1996). Prevalence of psychiatric disorders in young people in the care system. *British Medical Journal, 313* (7071), 1529-1530.

Miller, J. R. (1996). *Shingwauk's vision: A history of native residential schools.* Toronto: University of Toronto Press.

Millham, S., Bullock, R., Hosie, K. & Haak, M. (1981). *Issues of control in residential child-care.* London: HMSO.

Millham, S., Bullock, R., Hosie, K. & Haak, M. (1986). *Lost in care.* London: Gower.

Ministry for Children and Families. (1998). *Children's residential care standards.* Victoria: Crown Publications.

Ministry of Children and Family Development. (2002). *A system of care.* A working paper of the system of care working group. Victoria: Ministry of Children and Family Development.

Ministry of Social Services. (1994). *Child, family and community service act.* Victoria: Crown Publications.

Ministry of Social Services. (1995, February). *Family and children's services factbook.* Victoria: Ministry of Social Services.

Mintzberg, H. (1989). Crafting strategy. *The Child and Youth Care Administrator, 2* (1), 28-39.

Osborne, S. P. (1992). The quality dimension. Evaluating quality of service and quality of life in human services. *British Journal of Social Work, 22*, 437-453.

Palmer, S. (1976). *Children in long-term care: Their experiences and progress.* Ottawa: National Department of Health and Welfare.

Papanek, E. (1972). Special report on the International Association of Workers for Maladjusted Children. *Child Care Quarterly, 1*(2), 139-146.

Parker, R. A. (1988). An historical background to residential care. In: Sinclair, I. (Ed.), *Residential care: The research reviewed* (pp. 1-38). London: HMSO.

Parker, R., Ward, H., Jackson, S., Aldgate, J. & Wedge, P. (Eds.). (1991). *Looking after children: Assessing outcomes in child care.* London: HMSO.

Phillips, D. & Maslowsky, B. (1993). Child and youth care and the Canadian youth justice system. In C. Denholm, R. V. Ferguson & A. Pence (Eds.), *Professional child and youth care in Canada* (pp. 44-78) (Second Edition). Vancouver: UBC Press.

Polanyi, M. (1958). *Personal knowledge: Towards a post-critical philosophy.* London: Kegan Paul.

Polnay, L. & Ward, H. (2000). Promoting the health of looked after children. *British Medical Journal, 320* (7236), 661-662.

Polsky, H. (1962). *Cottage six: The social systems of delinquent boys in residential treatment.* New York: Russell Sage.

Polsky, H. & Claster, D. S. (1968). *The dynamics of residential treatment: A social system analysis.* Chapel Hill: University of North Carolina Press.

Polsky, H., Claster, D. S. & Goldberg, C. (Eds.). (1970). *Social system perspectives in residential institutions.* East Lansing: Michigan State University Press.

Prosser, H. (1976). *Perspectives on residential child care: An annotated bibliography.* Windsor: NFER Publishing.

Pugh, G. & De'Ath, E. (1994). *The needs of parents: Practice and policy in parent education.* Basingstoke: Macmillan.

Quality Assurance Agency for Higher Education. (2000). *Social policy and administration, and social work.* Gloucester: Quality Assurance Agency for Higher Education.

Rae-Grant, Q. & Moffat, P. J. (1971). *Children in Canada: Residential care.* Toronto: Leonard Crainford.

Raychaba, B. (1988). *To be on our own with no direction from home.* Ottawa: National Youth in Care Network.

Raychaba, B. (1993). *Pain . . . lots of pain.* Ottawa: National Youth in Care Network.

Reason, P. & Rowan, J. (1981). *Human inquiry: A sourcebook of new paradigm research.* New York: Wiley.

Reay, R. (1986). Bridging the gap: A model for integrating theory and practice. *British Journal of Social Work, 16*, 65-77.

Redl, F. (1959). Strategy and techniques of the life space interview. *American Journal of Orthopsychiatry, 29*, 1-18.

Redl, F. & Wineman, D. (1951). *Children who hate: The disorganization and breakdown of behavior controls.* Glencoe, IL: Free Press.

Redl, F. & Wineman, D. (1952). *Controls from within: Techniques for the treatment of the aggressive child.* Glencoe, IL: Free Press.

Reichertz, D. (1978). *Residential care: The impact of residential policies, structures and staff on resident children.* Montreal: McGill University.

Reinharz, S. (1992). *Feminist methods in social research.* New York: Oxford University Press.

Rowe, J. & Lambert, L. (1973). *Children who wait.* London: Association of British Adoption Agencies.

Rubin, S. (1972). Children as victims of institutionalisation. *Child Welfare, 51*(1), 6-18.

Rutter, M. (1975). *Helping troubled children.* Hammondsworth, England: Penguin.

Savicki, V. & Brown, R. (1985). *Working with troubled children.* New York: Human Sciences Press.

Schon, D. A. (1983). *The reflective practitioner: How professionals think in action.* New York: Basic Books.

Schur, E. M. (1973). *Radical non-intervention: Rethinking the delinquency problem.* Englewood Cliffs, NJ: Prentice-Hall.

Seita, J., Mitchell, M. & Tobin, C. (1996). *In whose best interest? One child's odyssey, a nation's responsibility.* Elizabethtown, PA: Continental Press.

Shamsie, J. (Ed.). (1977). *Experience & experiment: A collection of essays.* Toronto: Leonard Crainford.

Shealy, C. N. (1996). The "Therapeutic Parent": A model for the child and youth care profession. *Child and Youth Care Forum, 25*(4), 211-271.

Shostack, A. L. (1997). *Group homes for teenagers: A practical guide.* Washington, DC: Child Welfare League of America.

Sinclair, I. (Ed.). (1988). *Residential care: The research reviewed.* London: HMSO.

Sinclair, I. & Gibbs, I. (1998). *Children's homes: A study in diversity.* Chichester: Wiley.

Social Services Inspectorate, Department of Health. (1994). *Standards for residential child care services.* London: HMSO.

Steinhauer, P. D. (1991). *The least detrimental alternative: A systematic guide to case planning and decision making for children in care.* Toronto: University of Toronto Press.

Storch, D. (1988). The development of provincial standards. In G. Charles & P. Gabor (Eds.), *Issues in child and youth care practice in Alberta* (pp. 106-113). Lethbridge, Alberta: Lethbridge Community College.

Strauss, A. L. (1987). *Qualitative analysis for social scientists.* New York: Cambridge University Press.

Strauss, A.L. & Corbin, J. (1990). *Basics of qualitative research: Grounded theory procedures and techniques.* Newbury Park: Sage.

Thomas, G. (1975). *A community oriented evaluation of the effectiveness of child caring institutions.* Athens, Georgia: Regional Institute of Social Welfare Research, Inc.

Treischman, A., Whittaker, J. & Brendtro, L. (1969). *The other 23 hours: Child care work with emotionally disturbed children in a therapeutic milieu.* Chicago: Aldine.

Tri-Council. (1998). *Ethical conduct for research involving humans.* Ottawa: Medical Research Council of Canada, Natural Sciences and Engineering Research Council of Canada, and the Social Sciences and Humanities Research Council of Canada.

Turner, P. (1979). *Operational review: Children's and youth institutions.* Toronto: Ministry of Community and Social Services.

United Nations. (1989). *Convention on the rights of the child.* New York: UNICEF.

Vail, D. J. (1966). *Dehumanization and the institutional career.* Springfield, IL: Charles C. Thomas.

VanderVen, K. (1996). Toward a professional dead end or a dynamic process of professional development? The paradoxes of Shealy's "The Therapeutic Parent": A model for the child and youth care profession. *Child and Youth Care Forum, 25*(5), 297-304.

Wade, J. & Biehal, N. with Clayden, J. & Stein, M. (1998). *Going missing: Young people absent from care.* Chichester: Wiley.

Wagner, G. (1988). *Residential care: A positive choice.* Independent review into residential care (Wagner Committee), London: HMSO.

Ward, A. & McMahon, L. (1998). *Intuition is not enough: Matching learning with practice in therapeutic child care.* London: Routledge.

Ward, H. (Ed.). (1995). *Looking after children: Research into practice.* London: HMSO.

Whitaker, D., Archer, L. & Hicks, L. (1998). *Working in children's homes: Challenges and complexities.* Chichester: Wiley.

Whittaker, J. K. (1978). The changing character of residential care: An ecological perspective. *Social Service Review, 52* (March), 21-36.

Whittaker, J.K. (1979). *Caring for troubled children.* San Francisco: Jossey-Bass.

Whittaker, J. K. (2000). The future of residential group care. *Child Welfare, 79*(1), 59-74.

Whittaker, J. K. & Trieschman, A. E. (Eds.). (1972). *Children away from home: A source book of residential treatment.* Chicago: Aldine-Atherton.

Winnicott, D.W. (1986). *Home is where we start from: Essays by a psychoanalyst.* London: W.W. Norton.

Wolfensberger, W. (1972). *Normalization.* Toronto: National Institute on Mental Retardation.

Wolins, M. & Gottesmann, M. (Eds.). (1971). *Group care: An Israeli approach. The educational path of Youth Aliyah.* London: Gordon and Breach.

Wolins, M. & Piliavin, I. (1964). *Institution or foster family: A century of debate.* New York: Child Welfare League of America.

Wozner, Y. (1991). *People care in institutions: A conceptual schema and its application.* Binghamton, NY: Haworth.

Youll, P. J. & McCourt-Perring, C. (1993). *Raising voices: Ensuring quality in residential care.* London: HMSO.

Zaganelli, L. (1988). Standards, peer review and accreditation. In G. Charles & P. Gabor (Eds.), *Issues in child and youth care practice in Alberta* (pp. 114-127). Lethbridge, Alberta: Lethbridge Community College.

Index

abnormality, 125
Aboriginal children, 10
Act for the Prevention of Cruelty to
    and Better Protection of
    Children, 10
acting out behavior. *See* pain/pain-based
    behavior
adoption, 12
Agnew, Neil, 133
Aichhorn, August, 54,61,76,143-45
Ainsworth, F., 2,12
Alasuutari, P., 46,47
Alston, P., 76-77
anger
    See also pain/pain-based behavior
    of youth, dealing with, 107-8
anxiety, staff, 114-21
Artz, S., 41
assessments, 18
Association for Child and Youth Care
    Practice, 155
asylums, 9
attachment, 9,12,13

basic social process (BSP), 54
basic social psychological processes
    (BSPPs). *See* psychosocial
    processes
Before the Best Interests of the Child
    (Goldstein, Freud & Solnit),
    76
behavior management
    being responsive versus reactive,
    114-15
    challenge by choice, 116-18
    as core task, 108-9
    through active involvement, 120-21

    through reading young people's
    behavior, 118-20
    use of influence versus control for,
    115-16
behavior problems
    See also pain/pain-based behavior
    due to psychoemotional pain,
    109-10
    motivation for, 119
    types of, 83-84
Berridge, David, 13,136-39
Bettelheim, B., 65
Blumer, H., 49
boarding school residences, 5
Bowlby, J., 9,12,13
Brendtro, L., 145-46
British Columbia, child welfare system
    in, 8-9
Brodie, I., 138-39
Brown, E., 139-40
Bullock, R., 134, 139-40

care
    behavior management as core task
    of, 108-9
    continuity of, 13
    ensuring quality of, 18-21
    policies, 153-55
    term usage, 97
care workers
    See also staff
    commitment of, 126-27,129-30
    competencies for, 156-60
    education of, 84-86,113-14,155-60
    overview of, 84-86
    as role models, 102
    supervision of, 104-5
    as surrogate parents, 15-17